The Seagull Sartre Library

The Seagull Sartre Library

The Seagull Sartre Library

VOLUME 3
ON POETRY

JEAN-PAUL SARTRE

TRANSLATED BY
CHRIS TURNER

Seagull
BOOKS

LONDON NEW YORK CALCUTTA

This work is published with the support of
Institut français en Inde – Embassy of France in India

✳

Seagull Books, 2021

Originally published in Jean-Paul Sartre,
Situations I © Éditions Gallimard, Paris, 1947, and
Situations III © Éditions Gallimard, Paris, new edition, 2003

These essays were first published in English translation by Seagull
Books in *The Aftermath of War* (2008) and *Critical Essays* (2010)

English translation © Christ Turner, 2008, 2010

ISBN 978 0 8574 2 906 3

British Library Cataloguing-in-Publication Data
A catalogue record for this book is available
from the British Library

Typeset by Seagull Books, Calcutta, India
Printed and bound in the USA by Integrated Books International

CONTENTS

❊

BLACK ORPHEUS[1]

What were you hoping, when you removed the gags that stopped up these black mouths? That they would sing your praises? Did you think, when the heads our fathers had ground into the dust had raised themselves up again, you would see adoration in their eyes? Here are black men standing, men looking at us, and I want you to feel, as I do, the shock of being seen. For, the white man has, for three thousand years, enjoyed the privilege of seeing without being seen. He was pure gaze; the light of his eyes drew everything out of its native shade; the whiteness of his skin was another gaze, was condensed light. The white man, white because he was a man, white as day, white as truth, white as virtue, lit up Creation like a torch, revealed the secret, white essence of other creatures.

1 First published as the introduction to Léopold Sédar Senghor, *Anthologie de la nouvelle poésie nègre et malgache* (Paris: Presses universitaires de France, 1948). Where the poems cited are extracted from this anthology, I give the references in the form: A, page number.

These black men look at us today and our gaze is driven back into our eyes; black torches light the world in their turn, and our white faces are now just little Chinese lanterns swaying in the wind. A black poet, without even a thought for us, whispers to the woman he loves:

> Naked woman, black woman
> Dressed in your colour which is life . . .
> Naked woman, dark woman!
> Ripe fruit with firm flesh, dark ecstasies
> of black wine.[2]

And our whiteness seems to us a strange pale varnish preventing our skin from breathing, a white undergarment, threadbare at the elbows and knees, beneath which, could we but divest ourselves of it, you would find real human flesh, flesh the colour of dark wine. We thought ourselves essential to the world, the suns of its harvests, the moons of its tides: we are merely beasts among its fauna. Not even beasts:

> These Gentlemen of the City
> These proper Gentlemen
> Who no longer know how to dance
>   by the light of the moon
> Who no longer know how to walk
>   on the flesh of their feet

---

2 Senghor, 'Femme noire', *Chants d'ombre* (A, 151).

Who no longer know how to tell tales
    around the fire . . .[3]

We, who were once divine-right Europeans, were already feeling our dignity crumbling beneath the gaze of the Americans and Soviets; Europe was already nothing more than a geographical accident, the peninsula Asia juts out into the Atlantic. At least we were hoping to recover a little of our grandeur in the menial eyes of the Africans. But there are no menial eyes any longer: there are wild, free gazes that judge our earth.

Here is a black man wandering:

to the end of
the eternity of their
cop-ridden boulevards . . .[4]

Here, another crying to his brothers:

Alas! Alas! Spidery Europe moves its fingers
and its phalanxes of ships . . .[5]

And here,

    the insidious silence of this European night . . .[6]

where

3 Guy Tirolien, 'Prière d'un petit enfant nègre' (A, 87).

4 Léon-G. Damas, 'Un clochard m'a demandé dix sous', *Pigments* (A, 14).

5 Aimé Césaire, 'Et les chiens se taisaient', *Les armes miraculeuses*.

6 Senghor, 'A l'appel de la race de Saba' (A, 152).

. . . there is nothing time does not dishonour.

A Negro writes:

> Montparnasse and Paris, Europe and its
> endless torments
> Will haunt us sometimes like a memory or a
> malaise . . .[7]

and suddenly France seems exotic to our own eyes. It is no more now than a memory, a malaise, a white mist that lingers in sun-drenched souls, a tormented hinterland unpleasant to live in; it has drifted north, it is anchored off Kamchatka: it is the sun that is essential, the sun of the tropics and the sea 'flea-ridden with islands' and the roses of Imanga and the lilies of Iarivo and the volcanoes of Martinique. Being is black, Being is fiery, we are accidental and distant, we have to justify *our* ways, our technologies, our half-baked pallor and our verdigris vegetation. By these calm, corrosive eyes we are gnawed to the bone:

> Listen to the white world
> horribly weary from its immense effort
> its rebel joints cracking beneath the hard stars,
> its blue steel rigidities piercing the mystic flesh
> listen to its deceptive victories trumpeting its
>   defeats

---

7 Jaques Rabémananjara, 'Lyre à sept cordes (Cantate)' (A, 201).

listen to the grandiose alibis for its lame stumbling
Pity for our all-knowing, naive conquerors.[8]

We are *done for*. Our victories, upturned, expose their
entrails, our secret defeat. If we want to break down this
finitude that imprisons us, we can no longer count on
the privileges of our race, our colour, our technologies:
only by tearing off our white under-garments to attempt
simply to be human beings shall we be able to rejoin that
totality from which these black eyes exile us.

Yet if these poems shame us, they do so inadver-
tently: they were not written for us. All the colonialists
and their accomplices who open this book will have the
impression that they are reading over someone else's
shoulder, reading letters not addressed to them. It is to
black people that these black people speak and they do
so to talk to them of black people: their poetry is neither
satirical nor imprecatory: it is a *gaining of awareness*. 'So,'
you will say, 'of what interest is it to us other than doc-
umentary? We can't enter into it.' I would like to indicate
the route by which we can gain access to this jet-black
world, and show that this poetry, that seems at first
racial, is ultimately a song of all for all. In a word, I am
speaking here to the whites and I would like to explain
to them what black people know already: why it is necessarily through a poetic experience that the black person, in his present situation, must first become aware of

8 Césaire, 'Cahier d'un retour au pays natal' (A, 59).

himself and, conversely, why black French-language poetry is the only great revolutionary poetry of today.

It is not by chance that the white proletariat seldom employs poetic language to speak of its sufferings, its anger or its pride in itself. I do not believe that the workers are less 'gifted' than our well-heeled young men: 'talent', that efficacious grace, loses all meaning when we claim to ascribe it more to one class than to another. Nor is it the case that the harshness of their labour deprives them of the strength to sing: slaves toiled even harder and we are familiar with slave songs. We have, then, to acknowledge the fact: it is the current circumstances of the class struggle that deter the worker from expressing himself poetically. Being oppressed by technology, it is a technician he wishes to become because he knows that technology will be the instrument of his liberation. If he is to be able one day to control the management of enterprises, he knows that only professional, economic, scientific knowledge will take him there.

Of what poets have dubbed nature he has a deep, practical knowledge, but it comes to him more through his hands than his eyes. Nature for him is Matter, that passive resistance, that inert, insidious adverse force to which he applies the instruments of his labour; Matter does not sing. At the same time, the present phase of his struggle calls for continuous, positive action: political calculation, exact prediction, discipline, mass organization;

dreaming would be treason here. Rationalism, materialism, positivism—these great themes of his daily battle
are the least conducive to the spontaneous creation of
poetic myths. The last of these myths, the famous 'new
dawn', has retreated before the necessities of the struggle:
the most urgent tasks have to be attended to; a particular
position has to be won, then another; a wage has to be
raised, a solidarity strike or a protest against the war in
Indo-china decided: effectiveness alone counts. And,
without a doubt, the oppressed class has first to gain self-
awareness. But this awareness is precisely the opposite of
a descent into selfhood: it is a question of recognizing,
in and through action, the objective situation of the proletariat that can be defined by the circumstances of the
production or distribution of goods. United and simpli-
fied by an oppression exerted on each and all, and by a
common struggle, workers know little of the internal
contradictions that nourish the work of art and are detri-
mental to praxis. For them, to know themselves is to situate themselves in relation to the great forces around
them; it is to determine the exact place they occupy
within their class and the function they fulfil within the
Party. The very language they use is free from the minor
slackenings of order, the constant, mild impropriety and
transmissive play that create the poetic Word. In their
jobs they employ precisely determined technical terms.
As for the language of the revolutionary parties, Parain
has shown that it is pragmatic: it serves to deliver orders,
slogans, information. If it loses rigour, the party falls

apart. All this conduces towards the ever more thorough-going elimination of the human subject. Poetry, by contrast, has to remain subjective in some way. The proletariat has not had a poetry that was both social and yet drew its sources from subjectivity, a poetry that was social to the very extent that it was subjective, that was founded on a failure of language and yet was as stirring, as widely understood as the most precise of slogans or as the 'Proletarians of all Countries, Unite!' that one finds over the gateways of Soviet Russia. Failing this, the poetry of the future revolution has remained in the hands of well-intentioned young bourgeois who drew their inspiration from their psychological contradictions, from the antinomy between their ideals and their class, from the uncertainty of the old, bourgeois language.

The Negro, like the white worker, is a victim of the capitalist structure of our society; this situation reveals to him his close solidarity, beyond nuances of skin colour, with certain classes of Europeans who are oppressed as he is; it prompts him to plan for a society without privilege, where skin pigmentation will be regarded as a mere accident. But, though oppression is oppression, it comes in different forms, depending on history and geographical conditions: the black man is its victim *as black man*, as colonized native or transported African. And since he is oppressed in, and on account of, his race, it is of his race that he must first gain awareness. He has to force those who, for centuries, have, because he was a Negro, striven in vain to reduce him to the animal state, to recognize him as a human being. Now, no 'way out' offers itself to him here, no deception or 'crossing of the floor': a Jew, who is a white man among white men, can deny that he is Jewish and declare himself a human being among human beings. The Negro cannot deny he is a Negro, nor lay claim to that colourless abstract humanity: he is black. He is, in this way, forced into authenticity: insulted and enslaved, he stands tall, picks up the word 'Negro' that is thrown at him like a stone and proudly, standing up against the white man, claims the name 'black' as his own. The final unity that will bring all the oppressed together in a single struggle must be preceded in the colonies by what I shall term the moment of separation or negativity: this anti-racist racism is the only path that can lead to the abolition of racial differences. How could it be otherwise? Can blacks count on the assistance of the distant white proletariat, its attention diverted by its own struggles, before they are united and organized on their own soil? And does it not, in fact, take a thorough analysis to perceive the identity of deep interests beneath the manifest difference of conditions? Despite himself, the white worker benefits a little from colonization: however low his standard of living, it would be even lower without it. In any event, he is less cynically exploited than the day-labourer in Dakar or Saint-Louis. And then the technical installations and industrialization of the European countries make it possible to regard socialization measures as immediately applicable there; seen from Senegal or the

Congo, socialism appears, first and foremost, as a pleasant fancy: for black peasants to discover that it is the necessary outcome of their immediate, local demands, they have first to learn to formulate those demands together and, therefore, to think of themselves as blacks.

But this consciousness differs in nature from the consciousness Marxism attempts to awaken in the white worker. The European workers' class consciousness centres on the nature of profit and surplus-value, on the current conditions of the ownership of the instruments of labour—in short, on the objective characteristics of their *situation*. By contrast, since the contempt whites display for blacks—which has no equivalent in the attitude of bourgeois towards the working class—aims to reach into the depths of their hearts, Negroes have to pit a more just view of black *subjectivity* against that contempt; race consciousness is, therefore, centred first on the black soul or, rather, since the term recurs often in this anthology, on a certain quality common to the thoughts and behaviour of Negroes which is termed *negritude*.

Now, to form racial concepts, there are only two ways of operating: either one can convert certain subjective characteristics into something objective or one can attempt to internalize objectively identifiable behaviours. Thus the black man who lays claim to his negritude in a revolutionary movement places himself initially on the terrain of Reflection, either wanting to rediscover in himself certain traits that are objectively observed in

African civilizations or hoping to discover the black Essence in the depths of his heart. It is in this way that subjectivity reappears, the subjectivity that is one's own relation to selfhood, the source of all poetry, which the worker has, in self-mutilation, cast off. The black man who calls on his coloured brethren to acquire a consciousness of themselves will try to present them with the exemplary image of their negritude and delve into his soul to grasp it. He wants to be at once a beacon and a mirror; the first revolutionary will be the proclaimer of the black soul, the harbinger who will wrench negritude from himself to hold it out to the world; he will be half-prophet, half-partisan—in short, a poet in the precise sense of the word, *vates*. And black poetry has nothing in common with the outpourings of the heart: it is functional, it meets a need that defines it exactly. Leaf through an anthology of today's white poetry and you will find a hundred diverse subjects depending on the mood and concerns of the poet, his condition and his country. In the anthology I am introducing here, there is only one subject, which all the poets attempt to deal with, more or less successfully. From Haiti to Cayenne, there is a single idea: to *show* the black soul. Negro poetry is evangelical, it announces the good news of negritude regained.

However, this negritude, which they wish to summon up from their uttermost depths, does not fall, of itself, under the soul's gaze: in the soul, nothing is *given*.

Those heralding the black soul have attended the white schools, in accordance with that iron law that denies the oppressed any weapon but those they have themselves stolen from their oppressors. It was when it ran up against white culture that their negritude passed from immediate existence to the reflective state. But, as a result, they more or less ceased to live it. By choosing to see what they are, they have become split; they no longer coincide with themselves. And, conversely, it is because they were already exiled from themselves that they have found they have this duty to *show*. They begin, then, with exile. A twofold exile: the exile of their bodies offers a magnificent image of the exile of their hearts. Most of the time they are in Europe, in the cold, amid the grey masses; they dream of Port-au-Prince, of Haiti. But that is not enough: at Port-au-Prince they were already exiled: the slave traders snatched their forefathers from Africa and scattered them. And all the poems in this book (except the ones written in Africa) will offer us the same mystic geography. A hemisphere; right at the bottom, in the first of three concentric circles, stretches the land of exile, colourless Europe; then comes the dazzling circle of the islands and childhood, dancing around Africa; Africa, the last circle, the navel of the world, the hub of all black poetry, dazzling Africa, Africa afire, oily as snake's skin, Africa of fire and rain, torrid and dense, phantom Africa flickering like a flame between being and nothingness, truer than the 'eternal cop-ridden boulevards', but absent, its black rays disintegrative of

Europe, yet invisible and beyond reach—Africa, the *imaginary* continent. It is the extraordinary good fortune of black poetry that the concerns of the colonized native find clear, grandiose symbols that have only to be meditated on and endlessly delved into: exile, slavery, the Europe–Africa pair and the great Manichaean division of the world into black and white. This ancestral exile of bodies provides a metaphor for the other exile: the black soul is an Africa from which, amid the cold apartment blocks of white culture and technology, the Negro is exiled. Negritude, present but hidden, haunts him, brushes against him, he brushes against its silky wing, it flutters, stretching out within him as his deepest memory and his highest exigency, as his buried, betrayed childhood and the childhood of his race and the call of the earth, as the seething of the instincts and the indivisible simplicity of Nature, as the pure legacy of his ancestors and as the Morality that should unify his truncated life. But if he turns around to look it in the face, it goes up in smoke; the walls of white culture stand between him and it—*their* science, *their* words, *their* ways:

> Give me back my black dolls, so that I may play
> the naive games of my instinct with them
> remain in the shadow of its laws
> recover my courage
> my boldness
> feel myself
> a new self from what I was yesterday

yesterday

without complexity

yesterday

when the hour of uprooting came . . .

they have burgled the space that was mine.[9]

And yet one day the walls of the culture-prison will have to be broken down, one day he will have to return to Africa: in this way, within the *vates* of negritude, the theme of the return to the native country and the re-descent into the vivid Hades of the black soul are indissolubly mingled. Involved here is a quest, a systematic stripping-down and an *askesis*, accompanied by a continuous effort to delve deeper. And I shall term this poetry 'orphic' because this tireless descent of the Negro into himself puts me in mind of Orpheus going to reclaim Eurydice from Pluto. So, by an exceptional poetic felicity, it is by abandoning himself to trances, by rolling on the floor like a man possessed and under attack from himself, by singing his anger, his regret or his hatreds, by baring his wounds, his life torn between 'civilization' and the old black roots—in short, it is by displaying the greatest lyricism that the black poet most surely attains to great collective poetry. In speaking only of himself, he speaks of all Negroes: it is when he seems stifled by the serpents of our culture that he shows himself at his most revolutionary, for then he undertakes systematically to destroy what he has learned from Europe and that demolition

9 Damas, 'Limbe', *Pigments* (A, 9).

in spirit symbolizes the great future uprising through which black people will shatter their chains. A single example will suffice to throw light on this last remark.

At the same time as they were struggling for their independence, most ethnic minorities in the nineteenth century tried passionately to revive their national languages. To be able to *call* oneself Irish or Hungarian, you have doubtless to belong to a community that enjoys broad economic and political autonomy, but to *be* Irish, you also have to *think* Irish, which means, first and foremost, to think in the Irish language. The specific features of a society correspond exactly to the untranslatable expressions of its language. Now, what is likely dangerously to hold back the effort of black people to throw off our tutelage is the fact that the proclaimers of negritude are forced to frame their gospel *in French*. Scattered to the four corners of the earth by the slave trade, black people have no common language; to encourage the oppressed to unite, they have to resort to the words of the oppressor. It is French that will provide the black bard with the biggest audience among black people, at least within the bounds of French colonization. It is into this gooseflesh language, pale and cold as our skies, which Mallarmé described as, 'the neutral language *par excellence*, since the particular genius of this land demands that all over-vivid or riotous colour be toned down'—into this language that is half-dead for them—that Damas, Diop, Laleau and Rabéarivelo will pour the fire from their skies and their hearts. Through it alone can they communicate. Like the scholars of the sixteenth century who could understand each other only in Latin, black people can meet only on the booby-trapped terrain the white man has prepared for them. Among the colonized, the colonialist has arranged to be the eternal mediator; he is there, always there, even when absent—even in the most secret conventicles.

And since words are ideas, when the Negro declares in French that he is rejecting French culture, he takes with one hand what he rejects with the other; he installs the enemy's thinking machine in himself like a mechanical grinder. This would be of no importance, were it not for the fact that this syntax and this vocabulary, crafted in other times and distant climes, to meet other needs and refer to other objects, are unsuitable for providing him with the means for speaking of himself, his concerns and hopes. French language and thought are analytic. What would happen if the black spirit were, above all, a spirit of synthesis? The rather ugly term 'negritude' is one of the only black contributions to our dictionary. But if this 'negritude' is a definable, or at least describable, concept, it must be made up of other more elementary concepts, corresponding to the immediate data of Negro consciousness: where are the words that would enable us to refer to these? How well one understands the lament of the Haitian poet:

> This nagging heart, that matches neither
> My language nor my costume,
> And into which bites, like a clamp,

Borrowed feelings and European
Customs, do you feel this suffering,
This unrivalled despair
At taming, with the words of France,
This heart that came to me from Senegal?[10]

However, it is not true that black people express themselves in a 'foreign' language, since they are taught French from their earliest years and are perfectly at ease in it when they think as technicians, scientists or politicians. We should speak rather of the slight, but constant, gap that separates what they say from what they mean as soon as they speak of themselves. It seems to them that a northern spirit steals their ideas, gently inflects them, so that they mean more or less than they intended; that the white words soak up their thought the way sand soaks up blood. If they suddenly take control of themselves, gather their wits and step back from what is happening, they see the words lying *over against them* in their strangeness, half signs and half things. There is no way they will speak their negritude with precise, effective words that always hit their target. There is no way they will speak their negritude *in prose*. But everyone knows that this sense of failure with regard to language considered as a means of direct expression is at the origin of all poetic experience.

The speaker's reaction to the failure of prose is, in fact, what Bataille calls the holocaust of words. So long as we are able to believe that a pre-established harmony

---

10 Léon Laleau, 'Trahison' (A, 108).

governs the relations between words and Being, we use words without seeing them, with a blind confidence. They are sense-organs, mouths and hands, windows opened on the world. At the first failure, this easy chatter falls away from us; we see the whole system; it is nothing but a broken, upturned machinery, its great arms still waving to *signal* in the void. We judge at a stroke the mad enterprise of naming. We understand that language is, in its essence, prose; and prose, in its essence, failure. Being stands before us as a tower of silence; if we still want to pin it down, it can only be by silence: 'to evoke, in deliberate shade, the silenced object by allusive, ever-indirect words, reducing themselves to an equal silence.'[11] No one has better expressed the idea that poetry is an incantatory attempt to evoke Being in and by the vibratory disappearance of the word. By going further in his verbal impotence, by driving words to distraction, the poet helps us to sense enormous silent densities beyond this self- cancelling hubbub. Since we cannot stop speaking, we have to *make silence with language*. From Mallarmé to the Surrealists, the deep aim of French poetry seems to me to have been this self-destruction of language. The poem is a *camera obscura* in which each word bangs insanely into the next. Colliding in the air, they set each other on fire and fall in flames.

---

11 Stephen Mallarmé, 'Magie' in *Oeuvres complètes* (Paris: Gallimard, 1945), p. 400.

It is within this perspective that we have to situate the efforts of the black evangelists. To the colonialist's ruse, they reply with a similar, but opposite cunning: since the oppressor is present even in the language they speak, they will speak that language to destroy it. Today's European poet tends to dehumanize words in order to restore them to nature; the black herald, for his part, will *degallicize* them; he will pound them, break down their customary associations, join them together violently.

> With little rain-of-caterpillar steps,
> With little gulp-of-milk steps,
> With little ball-bearing steps
> With little seismic-shock steps
> The yams in the soil are taking great star-gap strides.[12]

He adopts them only when they have disgorged their whiteness, making this language in ruins a solemn and sacred super-language, Poetry. By Poetry alone, the blacks of Antananarivo, Cayenne, Port-au-Prince and Saint-Louis can communicate with each other unwitnessed. And since French lacks terms and concepts for defining negritude, since negritude is silence, to evoke it, they will use, 'allusive, ever-indirect words, reducing themselves to an equal silence'. Short-circuits of language: behind the words falling in flames, we glimpse a large, black, mute idol. It is not, then, simply the intention the Negro has

---

12 Césaire, 'Tam-tam II', *Les armes miraculeuses*, p. 156.

of depicting himself that seems to me poetic. It is also his own way of using the means of expression at his disposal. His situation prompts him to do so: even before he can think of singing, the light of the white words is refracted in him, polarized and altered. Nowhere is this more evident than in the use he makes of the coupled terms 'black/white', which cover both the great cosmic divide between night and day and the human conflict between the native and the colonialist. But it is a hierarchical couple: in delivering it to the Negro, the schoolteacher also delivers a hundred habits of speech that confirm the white man's precedence over the black. The Negro will learn to say, 'playing the white man' to indicate honesty, to speak of 'black looks' and the blackness of a soul or a crime. The moment he opens his mouth, he accuses himself, unless he makes an enormous effort to overturn the hierarchy. And if he overturns it *in French*, he is already being poetic: can you imagine the strange flavour expressions like 'the blackness of innocence' or 'the shades of virtue' would have for us? It is this we savour on each of the pages of this book and, for example, when we read:

Your breasts of black satin,
    curvaceous and gleaming . . .
this white smile
of your eyes
in the shadow of your face
awaken in me, this evening,

the muffled rhythms . . .
that inebriate
our black, naked sisters
over there in the land of Guinea
and stir in me
this evening
Negro twilights heavy with sensual feeling
for
the soul of the black country where
    the ancients sleep
lives and speaks
this evening
in the tremulous strength of your hollow
    loins . . .[13]

Throughout this poem, black is a colour or, rather, a light; its gentle, diffuse radiance dissolves our habitual perceptions: the black country where the ancients sleep is not a dark hell but a land of sun and fire. On the other hand, the superiority of the white over the black isn't merely an expression of the superiority the colonialist claims over the native: at a deeper level, it expresses the adoration of *daylight* and our dread of the night, which is also universal. In this sense, the black writers re-establish this hierarchy they have just overturned. They do not want at all to be poets of the *night*, that is to say, of vain revolt and despair. They are announcing a dawn; they are hailing 'the transparent dawning of a new day'.

---

13 Tirolien, 'L'âme du noir pays' (A, 87).

As a result, the black recovers, at their hand, its sense of gloomy presage. 'Negro, black as misery,' exclaims one of them, and another: 'Deliver me from the night of my blood.'

So the word black turns out to contain both the whole of Evil and the whole of Good; it recovers an almost unsustainable tension between two contradictory classifications: the solar and the racial hierarchies. From this it acquires an extraordinary poetry, like those self-destructive objects produced by Duchamp and the Surrealists; there is a secret blackness of the white, a secret whiteness of the black, a frozen flickering of being and non-being that is nowhere so well expressed perhaps as in this poem by Césaire:

> My great wounded statue a stone on its brow
> my great inattentive
> pitilessly flecked daylight flesh my great
> night-time flesh flecked with
> day[14]

The poet will go even further. He writes of 'Our faces handsome as the true operative power of negation.'[15]

Behind this abstract eloquence redolent of Lautréamont, one glimpses the boldest, most refined effort to give a meaning to black skin and achieve the poetic synthesis of the two faces of night. When Diop says of the

---

14 Césaire, 'L'irrémédiable', *Les armes miraculeuses*.

15 Césaire, 'Barbare', *Soleil cou coupé* (A, 56).

Negro that he is 'black as misery', he presents the black as pure privation of light. But Césaire develops this image and deepens it: the night is no longer absence, it is refusal. Black is not a colour; it is the destruction of that borrowed brightness that comes down to us from the white sun. The Negro revolutionary is negation because he seeks to be a pure stripping-bare: to construct his Truth, he has first to wreck others' truths. Black faces, these patches of night that haunt our days, embody the obscure work of Negativity that patiently gnaws away at concepts. So, by a turnabout that curiously recalls that of the humiliated, insulted Negro when he claims for himself the name of 'dirty nigger', it is the privative aspect of the darkness that establishes its value. Freedom is night-coloured.

Destruction, auto-da-fe of language, magical symbolism, conceptual ambivalence—the whole of modern poetry is here, from the negative standpoint. But this is not an arbitrary game. The situation of black people, their original 'tornness' and the alienation to which a foreign way of thinking subjects them in the name of assimilation oblige them to reconquer their existential unity as Negroes, or, if you prefer, the original purity of their projects, by a progressive *askesis* beyond the universe of discourse. Negritude, like freedom, is both starting point and final end: it is a question of shifting it from the immediate to the mediate, of *thematizing* it. The black person has, then, to die to white culture to be reborn to the black soul, in the same way as the Platonic philosopher dies to his body to be reborn to the truth. This dialectical, mystical return to origins necessarily implies a method. But that method does not present itself as a bundle of rules for the direction of the mind. It is one with the person applying it; it is the dialectical law of the successive transformations that will bring the Negro to coincide with himself in negritude. It is not, for him, a question of *knowing*, nor of wrenching himself out of himself in ecstasy, but of discovering and, at the same time, becoming what he is.

To this original simplicity of existence there are two convergent paths of access, the one objective, the other subjective. The poets in our anthology at times employ the one and at times the other. Sometimes they use both at once. There is, in fact, an objective negritude that is expressed in the mores, arts, songs and dances of the African peoples. The poet will prescribe for himself, as spiritual exercise, to allow himself to be fascinated by primitive rhythms and let his thought flow into the traditional forms of black poetry. Many of the poems gathered here are called 'tom-toms', because they borrow from the nocturnal drummers a percussive rhythm that is at times spare and regular, at others torrential and bounding. The poetic act is then a dance of the soul; the poet whirls like a dervish until he faints; he has attuned himself to the time of his ancestors, he feels its strange jolting rhythm; it is in this rhythmic flow that he hopes to find himself again. I will say that he is trying to give himself up to possession by the negritude of his people; he hopes the echoes of his tom-tom will awaken the immemorial instincts dormant in him. Leafing through this anthology, you will get the impression that the tom-tom is tending to become a genre of black poetry, as the sonnet and the ode were of ours. Others will take their inspiration, like Rabémananjara, from royal proclamations; yet others will draw on the popular source of the 'hainteny'. The calm centre of this maelstrom of rhythms, songs and cries is, in its naive majesty, the poetry of Birago Diop: it alone is at rest because it comes straight out of the tales of the *griots* and the oral tradition. Almost all the other attempts have something tense, forced and desperate about them, because they aim to return to folk poetry rather than emanating from it. But, however distant he is from the 'black country where the ancients sleep', the black poet is closer than us to the great age when, as Mallarmé puts it, 'the word creates gods'. It is almost impossible for *our* poets to reconnect with popular tradition: ten centuries of refined poetry separate them from it and, indeed, the folk inspiration has dried up; we could at best imitate its simplicity from the outside. By contrast, black Africans are still in the great period of mythic fecundity and black francophone poets do not merely amuse themselves with these myths as we do with our songs: they allow themselves to be entranced by them, so that at the end of the incantation, a magnificently evoked negritude emerges. This is why

I call this method of 'objective poetry' a weaving of spells or magic.

Césaire chose that his homeward journey would be made walking backwards. Since this Eurydice will vanish in smoke if the black Orpheus turns around to look at her, he will descend the royal road of his soul with his back turned to the far end of the cave; he will descend beneath words and meanings—'to think of you, I left all my words at the pawnbrokers'[16]—beneath daily behaviour and the plane of 'repetition', beneath even the first reefs of revolt, his back turned, his eyes closed, so as to be able, at last, to touch the black water of dreams with his bare feet and let him-self drown in them. Then desire and dream will rise up roaring like a tidal wave, will make words dance like driftwood, will throw them, pêle-mêle, shattered, on to the shore.

> Words transcend themselves, high and low
> permit of no distraction
> towards a heaven and an earth, the old geography
> is over and done
>   with too . . .
> By contrast, a curiously breathable tiering
> occurs, real, but
>   on one level. On the gaseous level of the
> organism, solid and liquid,
> white and black, day and night.[17]

---

16 Césaire, 'Le cristal automatique', *Les armes miraculeuses*.
17 Césaire, 'L'irrémédiable', *Les armes miraculeuses*.

We recognize the old Surrealist method here (for automatic writing, like mysticism, is a method: learning and practice must go into it; it must be set going). You have to plunge beneath the surface crust of reality, of common sense, of *la raison raisonnante*, to reach the bottom of the soul and awaken the immemorial powers of desire. Of the desire that makes man a refusal of everything and a love of everything, a radical negation of natural laws and of the possible, an appeal to miracles; of the desire which, by its mad cosmic energy, plunges man back into the seething bosom of nature by affirming his right to dissatisfaction. And Césaire is not the only Negro writer to take this path. Before him, Étienne Lero had founded *Légitime Défense*. 'More than a magazine,' says Senghor, '*Légitime Défense* was a cultural movement. Setting out from the Marxist analysis of the society of the "isles", it discovered the West Indian as the descendant of black African slaves, kept for three centuries in the stultifying condition of proletarian. It asserted that only Surrealism could deliver him from his taboos and express him in his wholeness.'

But, precisely, if we compare Lero to Césaire, we cannot but be struck by their dissimilarities, and the comparison may enable us to measure the abyss that separates white Surrealism from its use by a black revolutionary. Lero was the forerunner. He invented the exploitation of Surrealism as a 'miraculous weapon' and an instrument of research, a kind of radar that you beam out into the uttermost depths. But his poems are schoolboy efforts,

JEAN-PAUL SARTRE | 28

they remain strict imitations: they do not 'transcend themselves'. Indeed, they close up on themselves:

> The old heads of hair
> Stick the bottom of the empty seas to the branches
> Where your body is but a memory
> Where the spring is doing its nails
> The spiral of your smile cast into the distance
> On to the houses we want nothing of . . .[18]

'The spiral of your smile', 'spring . . . doing its nails'—we recognize here the preciosity and gratuitousness of the Surrealist image, the eternal practice of throwing a bridge between the two most distant terms, hoping, without too much conviction, that this 'throw of the dice' will deliver a hidden aspect of being. Neither in this poem nor in the others do I see Lero demanding the liberation of black people; at best, he calls for the formal liberation of the imagination. In this wholly abstract game, no alliance of words even distantly evokes Africa. Take these poems out of this anthology, conceal the author's name, and I defy anyone, black or white, not to attribute them to a European collaborator of *La Révolution Surréaliste* or *Le Minotaure*. This is because the aim of Surrealism is to recover, beyond race and condition, beyond class and behind the incendiary effects of language, a dazzling silent darkness that is no longer the

---

18 Lero, 'Châtaignes aux cils' (A, 53).

opposite of anything, not even daylight, because day and night and all opposites melt and vanish in that darkness. One might speak, then, of an impassibility, an impersonality of the Surrealist poem, just as there is an impassibility and an impersonality of the Parnassian movement.

By contrast, a poem by Césaire flares and whirls like a rocket; suns burst from it spinning and exploding into new suns; it is a perpetual transcendence. It is not about joining in the calm unity of opposites, but of making one of the contraries of the black/white couple stand up like an erection in its opposition to the other. The density of these words, thrown into the air like rocks by a volcano, is negritude defining itself against Europe and colonization. What Césaire destroys is not all culture, but white culture. What he brings out is not the desire for everything, but the revolutionary aspirations of the oppressed Negro. What he reaches to in the depths of his being is not spirit, but a certain form of concrete, determinate humanity. As a result, we can speak here of 'committed', even directed automatic writing—not that thought intervenes, but because the words and images perpetually express the same torrid obsession. In the depths of himself, the white Surrealist finds release from tension; in the depths of himself, Césaire finds the stiff inflexibility of protest and resentment. Lero's words are organized flabbily, relaxedly, by a loosening of logical connections, around vague, broad themes. Césaire's words are pressed up against each other and cemented by his furious passion. Between the most daring comparisons, the most distant terms, there runs a secret thread of hatred and hope. Compare, for example, 'the spiral of your smile cast into the distance', which is a product of the free-play of the imagination and an invitation to day-dreaming, with

> and the radium mines buried in the abyss of
> my innocences
> will leap as grains
> into the birds' feeding trough
> and the stere of stars
> will be the shared name of the firewood
> gathered from the alluvia of the singing
> seams of night

where the *disjecta membra* of the vocabulary arrange themselves to give us a glimpse of a black *Ars poetica*.

Or read:

> Our faces handsome as the true operative
> power of negation[19]

and then read:

> and the sea flea-ridden with islands
>   crunching between the fingers of
> the flamethrower roses and my intact body
> of one thunderstruck.[20]

---

19 Césaire, 'Barbare', *Soleil cou coupé* (A, 56).

20 Césaire, 'Soleil serpent', *Les armes miraculeuses* (A, 63).

We have here the transformation scene of the fleas of black destitution jumping around among the hair of the water, 'isles' lying in the light, crunching beneath the fingers of the heavenly de-louser, the rosy-fingered dawn, that dawn of Greek and Mediterranean culture, snatched by a black thief from the sacrosanct Homeric poems, its slave-princess' fingernails suddenly enslaved by a Toussaint Louverture to squash the triumphant parasites of the Negro sea, the dawn that suddenly rebels and metamorphoses, pours out fire like the savage weapon of the whites and, as a flame-thrower, weapon of scientists and torturers, strikes with its white fire the great black Titan, who rises intact and eternal to mount an assault on Europe and Heaven. In Césaire, the great Surrealist tradition comes to its end, assumes its definitive meaning and destroys itself: Surrealism, a European poetic movement, is stolen from the Europeans by a black man who turns it against them and assigns it a strictly defined function. I have stressed above how the entire proletariat closed their minds to this reason-wrecking poetry: in Europe, Surrealism, rejected by those who could have transfused their blood into it, languishes and withers. But at the very moment it is losing contact with the Revolution, here in the Antilles it is being grafted on to another branch of the universal Revolution; it is blossoming into an enormous dark flower. Césaire's originality lies in his having poured his narrow, powerful concerns as Negro, oppressed individual and militant into the world of the most destructive, most free, most metaphysical poetry, at a point when Éluard and Aragon were failing to give a political content to their verse. And finally, what is wrenched from Césaire like a cry of pain, love and hatred is negritude-as-object. Here again, he is continuing the Surrealist tradition which wants the poem to *objectify*. Césaire's words do not describe negritude; they do not refer to it; they do not copy it from the outside as a painter does with a model: they *make* it, they compose it before our eyes. From this point on, it is a thing you can observe and come to know. The subjective method he has chosen reunites with the objective method we spoke of above: he thrusts the black soul out of itself at the point when others are trying to internalize it. The final result is the same in both cases. Negritude is a distant tom-tom in the nocturnal streets of Dakar; it is a voodoo cry issuing from a basement window in Haiti, slithering out at street level; it is a Congolese mask, but it is also a poem by Césaire, slobbery, bloody, mucus-filled, writhing in the dust like a severed worm. This double spasm of absorption and excretion beats out the rhythm of the black heart on every page of this collection.

So what, at present, is this negritude, the sole concern of these poets, the sole subject of this book? The first answer must be that a white man cannot properly speak of this, since he has no internal experience of it and since European languages lack words that would enable him to describe it. I should, then, let the reader encounter it as he reads these pages and form the idea of it that he sees fit. But this introduction would be incomplete if, having

indicated that the quest for the black Holy Grail repre-
sented, in its original intention and its methods, the
most authentic synthesis of revolutionary aspirations and
poetic concern, I did not show that this complex notion
is, at its heart, pure Poetry. I shall confine myself, therefore, to examining these poems objectively as a body of
testimony and to cataloguing some of their main themes.
'What makes the negritude of a poem,' says Senghor, 'is
not so much the theme as the style, the emotional
warmth that lends life to the words, that transmutes talk
into the Word.' We could not be better warned that
negritude is not a state, nor a definite set of vices and
virtues, of intellectual and moral qualities, but a certain
affective attitude to the world. Since the early part of
this century, psychology has given up on its great
scholastic distinctions. We no longer believe mental facts
are divided into volitions or actions, cognitions or perceptions and blind feelings or passivities. We know a
feeling is a definite way of experiencing our relation to
the world around us and includes in it a certain understanding of that universe. It is a tensing of the soul, a
choice of oneself and others, a way of going beyond the
raw data of experience—in short a *project*, just like an
act of will. Negritude, to use Heideggerian language, is
the Negro's being-in-the-world.

This is how Césaire puts it:

my negritude is not a stone, its deafness
 hurled against the clamour of
the day

> my negritude is not a leukoma of dead liquid
> over the earth's dead eye
> my negritude is neither tower nor cathedral
> it takes root in the red flesh of the soil
> it takes root in the ardent flesh of the sky
> it breaks through the opaque prostration
> with its upright patience.[21]

Negritude is depicted in these fine verses far more as act than as disposition. But that act is an inner determination: it is not a question of *taking* the things of this world in one's hands and transforming them; it is a matter of *existing* amid the world. The relation to the universe remains an *appropriation*. But it is not a technical appropriation. For the white man, to possess is to transform. Admittedly, the white worker works with instruments he does not own. But at least his techniques are his own. If it is true that the major inventions of European industry are attributable to a personnel recruited mainly from the middle classes, at least the crafts of carpenter, joiner and turner still seem to them a genuine heritage, though the direction taken by large-scale capitalist production tends to divest even them of the 'enjoyment of their work'. But it is not enough to say that the black worker works with borrowed instruments; the techniques too are borrowed.

---

21 Césaire, 'Cahier d'un retour au pays natal' (A, 58–9). This translation by Clayton Eshleman and Annette Smith, from Aimé Césaire, *The Collected Poetry* (Berkeley: University of California Press, 1983), pp. 67–9.

Césaire calls his black brothers:

Those who have invented neither powder
    nor compass
those who could harness neither steam nor
    electricity
those who explored neither the seas nor the
    sky . . .[22]

This lofty claim to non-technicity reverses the situation: what could pass for a failing becomes a positive source of richness. The technical relation to nature discloses it as pure quantity, inertia, externality: it dies. By his lofty refusal to be *homo faber*, the Negro gives it back its life. As if, in the 'man–nature' couple, the passivity of one of the terms necessarily entailed the activity of the other. Actually, negritude is not a passivity, since it 'pierces the flesh of heaven and earth', it is a 'patience' and patience is seen as an active imitation of passivity. The action of the Negro is, first, action on himself. The black man stands and immobilizes himself like a bird-charmer and things come and perch on the branches of this false tree. This is indeed a harnessing of the world, but a magical harnessing through silence and stillness: by acting first on nature, the white man loses *himself* as he loses *it*; by acting first on himself, the Negro aspires to gain nature by gaining himself.

---

22 Césaire, *The Collected Poetry*, p. 67.

[They] yield, captivated, to the essence of all
things
ignorant of surfaces but captivated by the
motion of all things
indifferent to conquering, but playing the
game of the world
truly the eldest sons of the world
porous to all the breathing of the world . . .
flesh of the world's flesh pulsating with the
very motion of the world![23]

On reading these lines, one inevitably thinks of the famous distinction established by Bergson between intellect and intuition. And, indeed, Césaire calls us 'all-knowing, naive conquerors'. Of tools the white man knows everything. But the tool scratches the surface of things; it knows nothing of *durée*, of life. Negritude, by contrast, is an understanding through sympathy. The black man's secret is that the sources of his Existence and the roots of Being are identical.

If we wanted to provide a social interpretation of this metaphysics, we would say this was a poetry of farmers pitted against a poetry of engineers. It is not true, in fact, that the black man has no technology: the relation of a human group of whatever kind with the outside world is always technical in one way or another. And conversely, it seems to me Césaire is unfair: Saint-Exupéry's plane, which creases the earth like a tablecloth

---

23 Césaire, *The Collected Poetry*, p. 69.

beneath it, is an instrument of disclosure. But the black man is, first of all, a farmer; agricultural technique is 'upright patience'; it has confidence in life; it waits. To plant is to impregnate the earth; one then must remain still and attentive: 'each atom of silence is the chance of a ripe fruit' (Paul Valéry), every moment brings a hundred times more than the farmer gave, whereas, in the manufactured product, the industrial worker finds only what he put into it; the man grows alongside his corn; from one minute to the next he grows taller and more golden; attentive to this fragile swelling belly, he intervenes only to protect. The ripe corn is a microcosm because, for it to rise, it took the contributions of sun, rain and wind; an ear of wheat is at once the most natural of things and the most improbable piece of good fortune. Technologies have contaminated the white farmer, but the black one remains the great male of the earth, the sperm of the world. His existence is great vegetal patience; his work is the repetition year upon year of the sacred coitus. Creating and fed by what he creates. To plough, to plant, to eat is to make love with nature. The sexual pantheism of these poets is doubtless what will first strike the reader; it is in this respect that they connect with the phallic rites and dances of black Africans.

> Oho! Congo, lying on your bed of forests,
>   queen of subdued
> Africa. May the phalluses of the hills bear
>   your standard high,

> For you are woman by my head, by my
> tongue,
> You are woman by my belly[24]

writes Senghor. And:

> Now I shall ascend the soft belly of the
> dunes and the gleaming
> thighs of the day . . .[25]

And Rabéarivelo:

> the blood of the earth, the sweat of the stone
> and the sperm of the wind.[26]

And Laleau:

> Beneath the sky, the conical drum laments
> And it is the very soul of the black man
> Heavy spasms of rutting man, sticky lover's sobs
> Offending against the calm of evening.[27]

We are a long way here from Bergson's chaste, asexual intuition. It is no longer a question of merely being in sympathy with life, but of being in love with all its forms. For the white technician, God is first and foremost an engineer. Jupiter ordains chaos and lays down laws for it; the Christian God conceives the world by his

24 Senghor, 'Congo', *Éthiopiques* (A, 168).

25 Senghor, *Chant du printemps* (A, 166).

26 Rabéarivelo, 'Cactus', *Presque–Songes* (A, 189).

27 Laleau, 'Sacrifice' (A, 108).

understanding and creates it by his will: the relation of creature to Creator is never a fleshly one, except for some mystics whom the Church regards with great suspicion. And even then mystical eroticism has nothing in common with fertility: it is the entirely passive wait for a sterile penetration. We are *moulded* from clay: statuettes produced by the *hand* of the divine sculptor. If the manufactured objects around us could worship their creators, they would doubtless adore us as we adore the All-Powerful One. For our black poets, on the other hand, Being comes out of Nothing like a male member becoming erect; Creation is an enormous, perpetual giving-birth; the world is flesh and child of the flesh; on the sea and in the sky, on the sand-hills, the rocks and in the wind, the Negro rediscovers the downy softness of human skin; he strokes himself against the belly of the sand, the thighs of the sky: he is 'flesh of the flesh of the world'; he is 'porous to all breath', to all pollen; he is by turns the female of Nature and its male; and when he makes love with a woman of his race, the sexual act seems to him the celebration of the Mystery of Being. This spermatic religion is like a tensing of the soul, balancing two complementary tendencies: the dynamic sense of being an erect phallus and the more muted, patient, feminine feeling of being a growing plant. So negritude, at its deepest source, is an androgyny.

> There you are
> standing naked

> clay you are and remember it
> but you are in reality the child of this
> parturiant shadow
> that sates itself with lunar lactogenic
> then you slowly take the form of a cask
> on this low wall crossed by flower dreams
> and the scent of the resting summer
> feeling, believing that roots are growing at
> your feet
> and running and twisting like thirsting snakes
> towards some subterranean spring . . .[28]

And Césaire:

> Worn-down mother, leafless mother, you are
> a poinciana bearing only
> the seed pods. You are a calabash tree, and
> you are merely a host of
> gourds . . .[29]

This deep unity of plant and sexual symbols is certainly the most original feature of black poetry, particularly in a period when, as Michel Carrouges has shown, most white poets' images tend towards mineralizing the human. Césaire, by contrast, vegetalizes, animalizes sea, sky and stones. More exactly, his poetry is a perpetual coupling of women and men, metamorphosed into animals, plants and stones, with stones, plants and animals

---

28 Rabéarivelo, '10', *Traduit de la nuit* (A, 182).

29 Césaire, *Les armes miraculeuses* (A, 73).

metamorphosed into human beings. So the black poet
bears witness to the natural Eros; he manifests it and
embodies it. If we wanted to find something comparable
in European poetry, we would have to go back to
Lucretius, the peasant poet who celebrated Venus, the
mother-goddess, in the days when Rome was little more
than a great agricultural marketplace. In our own day, I
can think of hardly anyone but Lawrence with a cosmic
sense of sexuality. And, even then, that sense remains, in
his case, highly literary.

But though negritude seems, fundamentally, this
static outpouring, a union of phallic erection and vegetal
growth, this single poetic theme does not encompass it
wholly. There is another motif that runs through this
anthology like a major artery:

> Those who have invented neither powder
>   nor compass ...
> Know the furthest recesses of the land of
>   suffering.[30]

Against the white man's absurd utilitarian agitation, the
black man pits the authenticity he has derived from his
suffering. Because it has had the horrible privilege of
plumbing the depths of misfortune, the black race is a
chosen one. And though these poems are anti-Christian
through and through, one might, in this regard, speak

---

30 'Cahier d'un retour au pays natal' (A, 57–8). The second of these
lines precedes the first in the published poem.

of negritude as a Passion: the self-aware black sees himself in his own eyes as the man who has taken the whole of human pain upon himself and suffers for everyone, even the white man.

> Armstrong's trumpet which . . . on the Day
> of Judgement will speak
> man's pain.
> (Paul Niger)[31]

Let us note right away that this is in no way a resigned suffering. I spoke not so long ago of Bergson and Lucretius; I would be tempted now to quote that great adversary of Christianity, Nietzsche and his 'dionysianism'. Like the dionysian poet, the Negro seeks to penetrate beneath the brilliant fantasies of daylight and, a thousand feet beneath the Apollinian surface, he encounters the inexpiable suffering that is the universal human essence. If we were trying to be systematic, we would say that, insofar as he is sexual sympathy for Life, the black man merges with the whole of Nature and that he proclaims himself Man insofar as he is Passion of rebellious pain. We shall sense the basic unity of this twofold movement if we reflect on the ever-closer relationship psychiatrists are establishing between anxiety and sexual desire. There is but a single proud upsurge, which we can equally well describe as a desire, which plunges its roots into suffering, or a suffering that has driven itself like a

---

31 Paul Niger, 'Lune' (A, 104).

sword through a vast cosmic desire. This 'upright patience' evoked by Césaire is, in one single outpouring, vegetal growth, phallic erection and patience against pain: it resides in the very muscles of the Negro; it sustains the black bearer walking a thousand miles up the Niger in overpowering sun with a fifty-pound load balanced on his head. But if we can, in a sense, equate the fertility of nature with a proliferation of woes, in another sense—and this too is dionysian—this fertility, by its exuberance, goes beyond pain, and drowns it in its creative abundance that is poetry, love and dance. To understand this indissoluble unity of suffering, Eros and joy, one has perhaps to have seen the blacks of Harlem dancing frenetically to the rhythm of those 'blues' that are the most sorrowful tunes in the world. It is rhythm, actually, that cements these many aspects of the black soul; it is rhythm that communicates its Nietzschean lightness to those heavy dionysian intuitions; it is rhythm—tom-toms, jazz, the bounding movement of these poems—that represents the temporality of Negro existence. And when a black poet prophesies a better future for his brothers, he does so in the form of a rhythm that depicts to them their deliverance:

> What?
> a rhythm
> a wave in the night through the forests,
>   nothing—or a new soul
> a timbre

an intonation

a vigour

a dilation

a vibration which, by degrees, flows out in

the marrow, contorts in

its march an old slumbering body, takes it by

the waist and whirls

and turns

and vibrates in the hands, the loins, the sex,

the thighs and the

vagina . . .[32]

But one must go even further: this fundamental experience of suffering is ambiguous; it is through it that black consciousness will become historical. Whatever, in fact, the intolerable iniquity of his present condition, the Negro does not first refer to *it* when he proclaims he has plumbed the depths of human suffering. He has the horrible advantage of having known slavery. Among these poets, most of them born between 1900 and 1918, slavery, abolished half a century earlier, remains the most vivid of memories:

My todays each have eyes glowering on my

yesterdays

Eyes rolling with rancour, with shame . . .

I still feel my dazed condition of old

from

knotty blows with a rope from bodies

---

32 Niger, 'Je n'aime pas l'Afrique' (A, 100).

charred from toe to charred back
flesh killed by searing brands
arms broken 'neath the raging whip . . .[33]

writes Damas, the Guyanan poet. And Brière, the
Haitian adds:

. . . Often like me you feel old aches
reawaken after the murderous centuries,
And feel the old wounds bleed in your flesh . . .[34]

It was during the centuries of slavery that the Negro
drank his fill of the cup of bitterness; and slavery is a past
fact that neither our authors nor their fathers knew
directly. But it is an enormous nightmare and even the
youngest of them do not know whether they have properly awoken from it.[35] From one end of the earth to the
other, black people, separated from their colonizers by
languages, politics and history, share a collective memory. This comes as no surprise if we remember that, in
1789, French peasants were still subject to fearful panics
that went back to the Hundred Years' War. So, when
black people look back over their basic experience, it
suddenly appears to them in two dimensions: it is both
an intuitive grasp of the human condition and the still
fresh memory of a historical past. I am thinking here of

33 Damas, 'La complainte du nègre', *Pigments* (A, 10–11).

34 J.-F. Brière, 'Me revoici, Harlem' (A, 122).

35 And, indeed, what is the present condition of the Negro in
Cameroon or the Ivory Coast but slavery in the strictest sense of the
term?

Pascal who repeated tirelessly that man was an irrational combination of metaphysics and history—inexplicable in his grandeur if he rises above the clay, inexplicable in his misery if he is still as God made him—and that, to understand him, one needed recourse to the irreducible fact of the Fall. It is in this same sense that Césaire calls his race 'the fallen race'. And, in a sense, I can quite well see how one can compare a black consciousness with a Christian consciousness: the iron law of slavery evokes the law of the Old Testament, which rehearses the consequences of Sin. The abolition of slavery recalls that other historical fact: the Redemption. The suave paternalism of the white man after 1848 and that of the white God after the Passion are similar. Except that the inexpiable Sin the black person discovers in the depths of his memory is not his own, but that of the white man; the first fact of Negro history is, indeed, an original sin, but the black man is its innocent victim. This is why his conception of suffering is radically opposed to white dolorism. If these poems are, for the most part, so violently anti-Christian, this is because the religion of the whites appears even more as a mystification to the eyes of the Negro than it does to the eyes of the European proletariat: it wants him to share the responsibility for a crime of which he is the victim. It wants to persuade him that the abductions, massacres, rapes and tortures that have soaked Africa in blood are a legitimate punishment, are deserved ordeals. You may perhaps say that, on the other hand, it proclaims the equality of all before God.

Before God, yes. I read recently in *Esprit* these lines from a correspondent from Madagascar:

> I am as convinced as you that the soul of a Madagascan is of the same value as that of a white man . . . Precisely as the soul of a child is of the same worth before God as the soul of its father. And yet, dear Editor, you do not allow your car, if you have one, to be driven by your children.

Christianity and colonialism could not be more elegantly reconciled. Against these sophisms, the black man, by the mere deepening of his memory as one-time slave, asserts that pain is man's lot and, for all that, is still undeserved. He rejects with horror the depressive Christian attitude, its morose voluptuousness, its masochistic humility and all the tendentious promptings to resignation; he lives out the absurd fact of suffering in its purity, injustice and gratuitousness and discovers in it that truth unknown or concealed by Christianity: suffering contains its own rejection within itself; it is, in its essence, refusal to suffer, it is the shadow side of negativity; it opens on to revolt and freedom. By so doing, he *historializes himself*, insofar as the intuition of pain grants him a collective past and assigns him a future goal. Just a moment ago he was pure emergence into the present of immemorial instincts, pure manifestation of universal, eternal fecundity. Now he calls on his coloured brethren in quite a different language:

> Black hawker of revolt,
> you have known the paths of the world
> since you were sold in Guinea . . .
> Five centuries have seen you arms in hand
> and you have taught the exploiting races
> the Passion for freedom.[36]

There is already a black Chronicle: first, the golden age of Africa, then the age of scattering and captivity, then the awakening of consciousness, the sombre, heroic days of the great revolts, of Toussaint Louverture and the black heroes, the fact of the abolition of slavery—'unforgettable metamorphosis', says Césaire— then the struggle for ultimate liberation.

> You await the next call,
> the inevitable mobilization,
> for your war has known only truces,
> for there is no land where your blood has not
> flowed,
> no language in which your colour has not
> been insulted.
> You smile, Black Boy,
> you sing,
> you dance,
> you dandle the generations
> rising every hour,
> on the fronts of labour and hardship,

---

36 Jacques Roumain, 'Bois-d'Ebène' (A, 114).

who will rise up tomorrow against the
                    Bastilles,
against the bastions of the future
to write in every tongue,
on the clear pages of every sky,
the declaration of your rights neglected
for more than five centuries . . .[37]

This is a strange, decisive turn: *race* has transmuted into *historicity*, the black Present explodes and temporalizes itself, negritude inserts itself with its past and its future into Universal History. It is no longer a state, nor even an existential attitude, it is a becoming. The black contribution to the development of humanity is no longer a savour, a taste, a rhythm, an authenticity, a cluster of primitive instincts, but an undertaking that can be dated, a patient construction, a future. Not so long ago, it was in the name of ethnic qualities that the black man claimed his place in the sun; he now bases his right to life on his mission; and that mission, like the proletariat's, comes to him from his historical situation: because he has, more than all others, suffered from capitalist exploitation, he has, more than all others, the sense of revolt and the love of freedom. And because he is the most oppressed, when he works for his own deliverance he strives necessarily for the liberation of all:

Black messenger of hope
for you know all the world's songs

---

37 Brière, 'Black Soul' (A, 128).

from the songs of the building-sites by the
      Nile
in times out of mind . . .[38]

But can we still, after this, believe in the inner homo-
geneity of negritude? And how are we to say what it *is*?
At times it is a lost innocence that existed only in a distant past, at times a hope that will be realized only in the
radiant city of the future. At times it contracts in a
moment of pantheistic fusion with Nature and, at others, it expands to coincide with the whole history of
Humanity; it is, at times, an existential attitude and, at
others, the objective totality of black-African traditions.
Is it something one discovers? Is it something one creates?
After all, there are blacks who 'collaborate'; after all, Senghor, in the notes with which he has prefaced the work
of each poet, seems to distinguish degrees within negritude. Does the self-appointed proclaimer of negritude
among his coloured brethren invite them to become ever
more black or does he, rather, by a kind of poetic psychoanalysis, disclose what they are to them? And is that
negritude necessity or freedom? For the authentic Negro,
is it the case that his behaviour flows from his essence in
the same way as consequences flow from a principle, or
is one a Negro in the same way as a religious believer has
the faith—that is to say, in fear and trembling, in a state
of anxiety, perpetually remorseful at never being suffi-
ciently as one would like to be? Is it a fact or a value?

---

38 Roumain, 'Bois-d'Ebène' (A, 114).

The object of an empirical intuition or a moral concept? Is it something achieved by thought? Or does thinking poison it? Is it only ever authentic when unthought and immediate? Is it a systematic explanation of the black soul or a Platonic archetype that one approaches indefinitely without ever attaining it? Is it, for black people, like our common sense, the most widely shared thing in the world? Or does it descend on some like grace and choose its elect? The answer will no doubt come that it is all these things and many more besides. And I agree: like all anthropological notions, negritude is a flickering between 'is' and 'ought'; it makes you and you make it: it is pledge and passion at one and the same time. But there is something more serious: the Negro, as we have said, creates an anti-racist racism for himself. He in no way wishes to dominate the world: he wants the abolition of ethnic privileges wherever their source; he asserts his solidarity with the oppressed of all hues. The subjective, existential, ethnic notion of negritude 'goes over', as a result into the—objective, positive, exact—notion of proletariat. 'For Césaire,' says Senghor, 'the "white man" symbolizes capital in the same way as the "Negro" symbolizes labour. Through the black-skinned men of his race, he is hymning the struggle of the world proletariat.' This is easy to say, but less easy to conceive. And it is doubtless not by chance that the most ardent high priests of negritude are, at the same time, Marxist activists. But, even so, the notion of race does not exactly match that of class: the former is concrete and particular, the latter universal and abstract; the one derives from what Jaspers calls understanding, the other from intellection; the former is the product of a psycho-biological syncretism, the latter a methodical construction on the basis of experience. In fact, negritude is the weaker upbeat in a dialectical progression: the theoretical and practical affirmation of white supremacy is the thesis, the position of negritude as the antithetical value is the moment of negativity. But that negative moment is not sufficient in itself and the blacks who play on it know this very well; they know its aim is to prepare the synthesis or realization of the human in a society without races. Thus negritude is bent upon self-destruction; it is transitional, not final; a means, not an end. At the moment the black Orpheuses embrace this Eurydice most tightly, they feel her vanishing in their arms. A poem by Jacques Roumain, a black Communist, provides the most moving testimony of this new ambiguity:

> Africa I have retained a memory of you
> Africa
> you are in me
> Like the splinter in the wound
> like a tutelary fetish in the centre of the village
> make me the stone in your slingshot
> make my mouth the lips of your wound
> make my knees the broken columns of your
> degradation
> YET

> I want only to be of your race
> workers peasants of the world . . .[39]

With what sadness he holds on, for a moment, to what he has decided to cast off! With what human pride he will shed, for other human beings, his pride as Negro! The person who says both that Africa is in him 'like the splinter in the wound' and that he wants *only* to be one of the universal race of the oppressed, has not thrown off the hold of unhappy consciousness. One step more and negritude will disappear entirely: of what was the mysterious, ancestral seething of black blood, the Negro himself makes a geographical accident, the insubstantial product of universal determinism.

> . . . Is it all these things climate range space
> that create the clan the tribe the nation
> the skin the race and the gods
> our inexorable dissimilarity?

But the poet does not quite have the courage to take over this rationalization of the racial concept: we can see that he confines himself to questioning; beneath his will to union, a bitter regret shows through. A strange path this: hurt and humiliated, black people search in the very depths of themselves to recover their most secret pride, and, when they have at last found it, that pride contests itself: by a supreme act of generosity they abandon it, as Philoctetus abandoned his bow and arrows to

---

39 Roumain, 'Bois-d'Ebène' (A, 116).

Neoptolemus. So Césaire's rebel discovers at the bottom of his heart the secret of his revolts: he is of royal lineage.

> It's true there's something in you that has never been able to bow the knee, an anger, a desire, a sadness, an impatience, in short a contempt, a violence . . . and there's gold not mud in your veins, pride not servitude. A King, you were once a King.

But he immediately wards off this temptation:

> My law is that I run from an unbroken chain to the confluence of fire
>
> that sends me up in smoke, that purges me and sets me ablaze with
>
> my prism of amalgamated gold . . . I shall perish, but naked. Intact.[40]

It is perhaps this ultimate nudity of man—wrenching from him the cheap white finery that masked his black breastplate, before undoing, then rejecting, that breastplate itself—it is perhaps this colourless nudity that best symbolizes negritude: for negritude isn't a state; it is pure self-overcoming, it is love. It is at the point where it renounces itself that it finds itself; it is at the moment it agrees to lose that it has won: the coloured man and the coloured man alone can be asked to renounce the pride of his colour. He is the one walking the ridge between

---

40 Césaire, 'Et le chiens se taisaient', *Les armes miraculeuses*.

past particularism, which he has just ascended, and future universalism that will be the twilight of his negritude; the one who pushes particularism to its limits, to find in it the dawning of the universal. And doubtless the white worker, too, achieves consciousness of his class in order to deny it, since he wishes for the advent of a classless society: but, let me say again, the definition of class is objective; it encapsulates only the conditions of his alienation; whereas the Negro finds race at the bottom of his heart, and it is his heart he has to rip out. So, negritude is dialectical; it is not only, nor is it mainly, the flowering of atavistic instincts; it represents the transcendence of a situation defined by free consciousnesses. The painful and hope-filled myth of Negritude, born of Evil and pregnant with future Good, is as alive as a woman who is born to die and who senses her own death in the richest moments of her life; it is an unstable repose, an explosive fixity, a self-renouncing pride, an absolute that knows itself to be transitory: for at the same time as it announces its birth and its death-throes, it remains the existential attitude that is chosen by free men and lived *absolutely*, drained to the very dregs. Because it is this tension between a nostalgic past, of which the black man is not fully a part, and a future in which it will give way to new values, negritude decks itself in a tragic beauty that finds expression only in poetry. Because it is the living and dialectical unity of so many opposites, because it is a complex resistant to analysis, only the multiple unity of a song and this dazzling beauty of the poem, which Breton terms 'fixed-explosive', can manifest it. Because any attempt to conceptualize its different aspects would necessarily lead to showing its relativity, whereas it is experienced in the absolute by regal consciousnesses and, because the poem is an absolute, it is poetry alone that will enable us to pin down the unconditional aspect of this attitude. Because it is a subjectivity that assumes objective form, negritude must be embodied in a poem, that is to say in an objective subjectivity; because it is an archetype and a value, it will find its most transparent symbol in aesthetic values; because it is a clarion call and a gift, it can be heard and given only through the work of art, which is a call to the freedom of the spectator and absolute generosity. Negritude is the content of the poem, it is the poem as—mysterious and open, indecipherable and allusive—thing in the world; it is the poet himself. We must go even further: negritude, the triumph of narcissism and the suicide of Narcissus, tensing of the soul beyond culture, words and all psychical facts, luminous night of nonknowledge, deliberate choice of the impossible and of what Bataille terms 'torture', intuitive acceptance of the world and its rejection in the name of the 'law of the heart', a twofold contradictory postulate, protesting retraction and expansion of generosity, is, *in its essence*, *Poetry*. For once at least, the most authentic revolutionary project and the purest poetry emerge from the same source.

And if the sacrifice is one day consummated, what will happen? What will happen if black people, laying aside their negritude in favour of Revolution, no longer wish to see themselves as anything but proletarians? What will happen if they allow themselves to be defined by their objective condition alone; if they force themselves, in order to struggle against white capitalism, to assimilate white technics? Will the source of poetry dry up? Or, in spite of everything, will the great black river colour the sea into which it hurls itself? This does not matter: every age has its own poetry; in every age the circumstances of history elect a nation, a race or a class to take up the torch, creating situations that can be expressed or overcome only through poetry; and sometimes the poetic elan coincides with the revolutionary, and sometimes they diverge. Let us hail, today, the historic opportunity that will enable black people to:

> utter the great Negro cry with such firmness
>   that the world will be
> shaken to its foundations.[41]

---

41 Césaire, *Les armes miraculeuses*, p. 156.

*

MAN AND THINGS

If we come at the published work of Francis Ponge without preconceived notions, we are tempted at first to think that, out of a singular affection for 'things', he has undertaken to describe them with the resources to hand. That is to say, he has set about describing them with words, with all the words that there are, with worn-out, overused, eroded words, such as present themselves to the naive writer, a mere assortment of colours on a palette. But if we read attentively, we are quickly disconcerted. Ponge's language seems bewitched or enchanted. As the words disclose a new aspect of the named object to us, it seems they also elude our grasp; they are no longer precisely the docile, commonplace tools of everyday life and they reveal new aspects of themselves. As a result, reading *Le Parti pris des choses* often seems like a worried oscillation between word and thing, as though in the end we are no longer quite sure whether the word is the object or the object the word.

Ponge's original concern is *with naming*. He isn't—
or at least he isn't primarily—a philosopher and it isn't
his aim to convey things at all costs. But the first thing
he does is speak—and write. He has entitled one of his
books *La Rage de l'expression* and he refers to himself, in
Le Mimosa, as an ex-martyr of language.[1] He is a man of
45 who has been writing since 1919, which shows well
enough that he came to things by way of reflection on
the spoken word.

Let's be clear about this, however. You shouldn't
believe that he talks for the sake of it, that the objects of
his descriptions are themes to which he is indifferent, or
even that it was his troubles with words that led him to
his awareness of the existence of things. He himself says,
in *Le Mimosa*:

> I have deep down an idea [of the mimosa] that
> I have to get out . . . I wonder whether it might
> not be the mimosa that first aroused my sensu-
> ality . . . I floated in ecstasy on the powerful
> waves of its scent. So that each time the mimosa
> appears now in my interior or around me, it
> reminds me of all that and fades immediately
> . . . Since I write, it would be unacceptable for
> there not to be a piece by me about mimosas.[2]

1 Francis Ponge, 'Le Mimosa', in *La rage de l'expression* (Paris: Gallimard, 1976), p. 80.

2 Ponge, 'Le Mimosa', pp. 76–7.

That he doesn't come to things by chance couldn't be more clearly put. Those he speaks about are chosen. They have lived in him for many a year; they inhabit his being; they carpet his memory. They were present in him long before he had his troubles with words, long before he opted to write about them; they already scented him with their secret meanings. And his current effort is directed much more at fishing these teeming monsters from the depths of his being and at *conveying* them, than at determining their qualities after scrupulous observations. It is said that Flaubert told Maupassant, 'Stand in front of a tree and describe it.' The advice, if it were actually given, is absurd. The observer can take measurements—and that is all. The thing will always refuse to yield its meaning—and its being—to him. Ponge no doubt looks at mimosas; he looks at them attentively and at length. But he already knows what he is looking for. Pebbles, the rain, the wind and the sea are already within him as complexes—and it is these complexes he wants to bring to light. And if we wish to know why, instead of the commonplace Oedipus complex or inferiority complex—or perhaps *alongside* the inferiority complex—he defines himself by the pebble-complex, the shellfish-complex or the moss-complex, the answer must be that this is the way it is for each of us and that this is the secret of his personality.

Yet he was one of those whose literary vocation is characterized by a furious wrestling with language. Though he began by assimilating and digesting the world of things, it was the great flat space of words that he discovered first. Man is language, he says. And he adds elsewhere with a kind of despair, 'All is words.' We shall better understand the meaning of this sentence in a moment. For the present, let us simply note this bias towards considering man from the outside, as the behaviourists do. Nowhere in his work will there be any question of *thought*. What distinguishes man from other species is this objective act we name speech, this original way of striking the air and constructing a sound object around himself. Ponge will even *naturalize* speech by making it a secretion of the human animal, a slime comparable to the snail's. 'The true secretion common to the human mollusc man . . . : I mean LANGUAGE.'[3] Or, elsewhere, 'Shapeless molluscs . . . millions of ants . . . your only dwelling is the common vapour of your true blood: speech.'[4]

Ponge regards speech as a real shell that enwraps us and protects our nudity, a shell we have secreted that suits the softness of our bodies. In his view, the tissue of words is a real, perceptible existence: he sees words around him, around us. But this rigorously objectivist

---

3 Francis Ponge, 'Notes for a Sea Shell', in *The Nature of Things* (Lee Fahnestock trans.) (New York: Red Dust, 2000), p. 48. I have generally opted to use this translation, which, though its title is somewhat at variance with Ponge's, captures the tone of the collection well. [Trans.]

4 Francis Ponge, 'Des raisons d'écrire', in *Le Parti pris des choses, précédé de douze petits écrits et suivi de Proêmes* (Paris: Gallimard/nrf, 1972), pp. 162–3.

conception of discourse, this materialist conception, so to speak, is at the same time an unreserved commitment to language. Ponge is a humanist. Since to speak is to be a man, he speaks to serve the human by speaking. Such is the avowed origin of his vocation as a writer.

> Instead of those gigantic monuments that testify only to the grotesque disparity between his imagination and his person, . . .

> I wish that man applied himself through the ages to creating a shelter not much larger than his body, one involving all his imagination and reason, that he put his genius to work on appropriate scale rather than disproportion . . . In that light, I particularly admire certain restrained writers or composers, . . . above all the writers, because their monument is made from the true secretion common to the human mollusc.[5]

It is well and good to serve the human by speaking, but that still requires words that must lend themselves to the task. Ponge is of the same generation as Parain; he shares with him that materialist conception of language that refuses to distinguish the Idea from the Word; like him, in the aftermath of 1918, he experienced that sudden distrust of discourse, that same bitter disillusionment. I have tried to give the reasons for this elsewhere. It seems generally agreed there was a 'crisis of language' later on

---

5 Ponge, *The Nature of Things*, pp. 47–8 (spelling anglicized).

in the period 1918–30. The experimentation of the symbolists, the famous 'crisis of science', the theory of 'scientific nominalism' it inspired and Bergsonian critique had laid the ground for it. But the young people of the post-war years had need of more solid motives. There was the violent discontent of the demobilized, their maladaptedness to civilian life; there was the Russian revolution and the revolutionary agitation that spread almost everywhere throughout Europe; and, with the appearance of new, ambiguous realities that were neither flesh nor fowl, there was the dizzying devaluation of the old words that couldn't quite name these new realities, even though the very ambiguity of these forms of existence prevented new names being found for them. However this may be, not all the malcontents chose to level their anger at language. To do so, one first had to have accorded remarkable value to it. This was the case with Ponge and Parain. Those who believed they could unstick ideas from words were none too troubled, or applied their revolutionary energies in other directions. But Ponge and Parain had, from the outset, defined man by speech. They were caught like rats in a trap, because speech was now worthless. We can truly say in this case that they were in despair: their position denied them the slightest hope. We know that Parain, haunted by a silence that constantly eluded him, went first to the extremes of terrorism before returning to a nuanced rhetoric. Ponge's path was more tortuous.

His objection to language is, first and foremost, that it is the reflection of a social organization he abhors. 'Our first motive was probably disgust with what we are compelled to think and say.' In this sense, his despair was less total than Parain's. Whereas Parain thought he saw an original defect in language, there was a naturalistic optimism about Ponge that made him see words as vitiated by our form of society.

> With all due deference to *words* themselves, *given the habits they have contracted in so many obnoxious mouths*, it takes quite some courage to make the decision not merely to write, but even to speak.[6]

And:

> These stampedes of cars and lorries, these districts where no people reside, but only goods or the files of the companies that transport them . . . these governments of hucksters and traders, *we'd say nothing about it* if they didn't force us to take part . . . Alas, horror of horrors, the same sordid order speaks *inside ourselves*, because we don't have other words or other big words (or phrases, that is to say, other ideas) than those that daily usage in this coarse world has prostituted from time immemorial.[7]

---

6 Ponge, 'Des raisons d'écrire', in *Le Parti pris des choses*, p. 163.

7 Ponge, 'Les Écuries d'Augias', in *Le Parti pris des choses*, pp. 155–6.

As we can see, Ponge's objection isn't really to language, but to language 'as it is spoken'. Hence he has never seriously considered remaining silent. As a poet, he sees poetry as a general enterprise of *cleaning up* language, just as the revolutionary may, in a way, look to clean up society. Moreover, for Ponge, the two are the same: 'I shall only ever bounce back in the pose of the *revolutionary* or the *poet*.'[8]

Though he doesn't find the theoretical impossibility or formal contradiction in language that Parain saw in it, his position is scarcely more enviable at the beginning. For in short, since he wants nothing of silence—because silence is a word, an empty word, and perhaps a trap—all that he has with which to make himself heard are words that he abhors. What is he to do? Ponge first adopts the negative solution offered to him by the Surrealists of destroying words with words. 'Let us make words ridiculous through catastrophe,' he writes, 'the simple abuse of words.'[9] He has in mind a radical devaluation; this is a scorched earth policy. But what can it produce? Is it true we shall construct a silence in this way? This is doubtless speaking 'so as to say nothing'. But is it, ultimately, words we are destroying? Aren't we simply continuing the movement begun by the 'obnoxious mouths' we detest? Aren't we hounding the proper

---

8 Ponge, 'A chat perché', in *Le Parti pris des choses*, p. 159.

9 Ponge, 'Justification nihiliste de l'art', in *Le Parti pris des choses*, p. 124.

meanings out of words, only to find ourselves later with all names rendered equivalent, forced, amid the disaster, to go on speaking nonetheless? And indeed Francis Ponge didn't press on with this experiment. His particular genius led him elsewhere. The point for him was, rather, to wrest words from those who misuse them and to attempt to develop a new trust in words. As early as 1919 he glimpses a solution, which might be said to be based on the imperfection of the Word:

> Divine necessity of imperfection, divine presence, in written texts, of the imperfect, of defects[10] and of death, bring me your help too! May the *impropriety* of terms make possible a new induction of the human among signs that are already too detached from it, and too dry, pretentious and swaggering. May all abstractions be consumed from within and, as it were, melted by this secret heat of vice, caused by time, death and the flaws of genius.[11]

His objection to words is that they adhere too closely to their most commonplace signification, that they are both exact and impoverished. But, looking more closely, he distinguishes turgidities, accidental detachments and adventitious meanings in them—an entire

---

10 Sartre's published text has 'vide' here rather than the 'vice' of Ponge's text. I have reverted to Ponge's original, on the assumption that Sartre's version is merely a misprint or mistranscription. [Trans.]

11 Ponge, 'La Promenade dans nos serres', in *Le Parti pris des choses*, pp. 127–8.

secret, useless dimension produced by their history and the blunderings of those who have used them. Aren't there the elements, in this neglected depth, of a rejuvenation of terms? It isn't so much a question of emphasizing their etymological sense to refresh them, as Valéry does, or discovering a subjective side to them by which to appropriate them the more surely: we should, rather, see them with the eyes that Rimbaud turned on the 'absurd pictures',[12] grasp them at the very moment when man's creations warp and buckle and escape him by the secret chemistries of their significations. In short, we should catch at them and seize them when they are becoming *things*. Or, rather, since the most human and most constantly handled of words is always, from a certain angle, a thing, we should strive to grasp all words— with their meanings—in their strange materiality, with the signifying humus, dregs or residue that fill them. To this very day he remains obsessed with the materiality of the word:

> Oh human traces, at arm's length, Oh original sounds, monuments of art's infancy . . . mysterious objects and characters perceptible by two senses only . . . I want to have you loved for yourselves rather than for your meaning. To raise you at last to a nobler condition than that of mere designations.[13]

---

12 Arthur Rimbaud, *A Season in Hell* (Oliver Bernard trans.) (London: Penguin, 1995), p. 33.

13 Ponge, 'La Promenade dans nos serres', in *Le Parti pris des choses*, p. 128.

He wrote these words in 1919. And, in *Le parti pris des choses*, his most recent work, returning to this assimilation of words to a shell secreted by human beings, he delights in imagining these shells emptied, after the disappearance of our species, in the hands of other species that would view them as we view the shells on the seashore.

> Oh Louvre of the written word, which may per-
> haps after the demise of this race be inhabited
> by other proprietors—monkeys, for instance, or
> birds, or some superior being—just as the crus-
> tacean takes the place of the mollusc in the peri-
> winkle shell.[14]

Escaping, in this way, man who produced it, the word becomes an absolute. And Ponge's ideal is for his works, built out of word-things that will survive his age and perhaps his species, to become things in their turn. Should we see this merely as the consequence of a reso- lutely materialist attitude? I don't believe so. But it seems to me that I find in Ponge a desire shared by many writ- ers and painters of his generation: that their creation should be a *thing*, solely and precisely inasmuch as it was their creation.

This effort to shift the meaning of terms remained pure revolt still, so long as the half-petrified significations discovered beneath the superficial crust of common sense were not directed towards objects specific to them.

14 Ponge, 'Notes for a Sea Shell', in *The Nature of Things*, p. 48.

This was still a pure effort of negation. Did Ponge understand that a genuine revolutionary had to be constructive? Did he understand that, if it too was not used to *designate* things, the 'semantic density' of words was in danger of remaining up in the air? He wanted to 'offer everyone the opening of inner trap-doors, a journey into the density of (words) . . . a subversion comparable to that effected by plough or spade, when suddenly and for the first time millions of particles of earth, seeds, roots, worms and little insects are turned up that have previously been buried.'[15]

But—and this is perhaps the most important turning point of his thought—Ponge realized that one couldn't go on for long burrowing into words *without any purchase on things*; he turned away from the great Surrealist prattling which, in many cases, consisted merely in banging objectless words against one another. He could renew the meaning of words and fully appropriate their deep resources only by employing them to name *other things*. So, if it is to be complete, the revolution of language has to be accompanied by a re-routing of attention: discourse has to be wrested from its commonplace usage, our gazes turned towards new objects, and we have to render 'the infinite resources of the density of things . . . with the infinite resources of the semantic density of words.'[16]

---

15 Ponge, 'Introduction au galet', in *Le Parti pris des choses*, p. 176.
16 Ponge, 'Introduction au galet', in *Le Parti pris des choses*, p. 176.

What, then, will these new objects be? The title of Ponge's collection tells us. Things exist. We have to come to terms with this; we have to come round to their terms. We shall, then, abandon all-too-human discourse and set about speaking of things, of taking their side.[17] Of things: that is to say, of the inhuman. However, the term inhuman has two meanings. If I thumb through Ponge's book, I see he has written about pebbles and moss, which I clearly recognize as things, but also of the cigarette, a very human requisite, and of the young mother, who is a woman—and the gymnast, who is a man—and of the Restaurant Lemeunier, which is a social institution. If, however, I read the passages relating to these latter objects, I see that the gymnast,

> Rosier than nature, less agile than an ape, . . .
> lunges at the apparatus, driven by sheer zeal.
> Then with the top of his body held fast in the
> knotted rope, he interrogates the air like a worm
> half out of its mound.
>
> For a finish, he sometimes plummets from
> the rigging like a caterpillar, only to bounce
> back on his feet . . .[18]

17 The undifferentiated triple meaning of Ponge's title—*le Parti pris des choses*—shows us how he intends to draw on the semantic density of words. That title implies '*prendre le parti des choses*' [taking the side of things] against human beings; *prendre son parti de* [coming to terms with] their existence (against the idealism that reduces the world to representations); and making an aesthetic *parti pris* [bias or prejudice] of them.

18 Ponge, 'The Gymnast', in *The Nature of Things*, p. 39 (translation modified).

The thing I immediately note is Ponge's effort to eliminate the privileged status accorded to the *head*, the human being's most human organ. For the rest of us, it is the soul of a person, or a little image of the soul perched atop the collar, and a separate entity. But Ponge restores it to the body; he no longer calls it head or face or countenance—these words are too fraught with human meaning, loaded as they are with smiles, tears or knittings of the brow—but 'the top of his body'. And if he compares the gymnast's body to a worm, he does so in order to eliminate the differentiation of the organs, by forcing upon us the image of the smoothest, least differentiated of creatures, so that the head becomes a mere questioning movement on top of an annelid. However, the trick of this description lies, mainly, in Ponge showing us the gymnast as the representative of an animal species. He describes him the way Buffon did the horse or the giraffe. What has been acquired by effort, he presents to us as a congenital property of the species. 'Less agile than an ape', he says—and these words are enough to transform this acquired skill into a kind of innate gift. In the end, he breaks down the artist's 'performance' into a series of behaviour patterns fixed by heredity, succeeding each other in a monotonous, meaningless order.

And now let us take the 'young mother':

Her face, often bent over her chest, grows slightly longer.

Her eyes, attentively peering down at a nearby object, occasionally look up, faintly distracted.

Their gaze is filled with confidence, but seeking continuation. Her arms and hands bend together in a crescent, mutually sustaining. Her legs, grown thin and weakened, are gladly seated, knees drawn up high. The distended belly, livid, still very tender; the abdomen readjusts to rest, to nights under covers.

. . . But soon up and about, the tall body moves in cramped fashion . . .[19]

In this case, the organs are separated out from each other and lead a slow-motion life, each in their turn. The human unity has vanished and we have before us not so much a woman as a polypary. And then, in the last lines, everything is gathered together. And the result is not a person, but a great, blind body.

Here, then, we have a mother and a trapeze artist turned to stone. They are *things*. All it took to achieve this result was to look at them without that human bias that freights human faces and actions with signs. There has been a refusal to stick the traditional labels of 'high' and 'low' on their backs, to presume that they have consciousness, to regard them, in short, as witch dolls. In a word, they have been seen through the eyes of behaviourists. And, with that, they are suddenly part of Nature once more; the gymnast, somewhere between ape and squirrel, becomes a *natural* product; the young mother is a higher mammal who has given birth.

---

19 Ponge, 'The Young Mother', in *The Nature of Things*, p. 40 (translation modified).

We have now understood that any kind of object will appear as a thing as soon as we have taken care to divest it of the all too human significations initially bestowed upon it. The project may actually seem an ambitious one: how am I, who am a man, to catch sight of a Nature without human beings? I once knew a little girl who would stamp noisily out of her garden and then tiptoe back in 'to see what it looked like when she wasn't there'. But Ponge isn't so naive as that: he is fully aware that his plan of getting down to the bare thing is merely an ideal.

> It is to the mimosa itself (sweet illusion!) that we now must come; if you like, to the mimosa without me . . .[20]

He writes elsewhere that he would like, 'to describe things from their own point of view, but this is, as end-point or perfection, impossible. There is always *some* relation to human beings . . . It is not things that speak among themselves, but human beings who speak among themselves about things, and it is not in any way possible to step outside the human.'[21]

We shall have to limit ourselves, then, to better and better approximations. And what we are entitled to do immediately is to divest things of their *practical* significations. Speaking of the pebble, Ponge writes:

> Compared to the finest gravel, one can say that given the place where it is found, and because

---

20 Ponge, 'Le Mimosa', in *La rage de l'expression*, p. 77.
21 Ponge, 'Raisons de vivre heureux', in *Le Parti pris des choses*, p. 167.

man is not in the habit of putting it to practical
use, the pebble is rock still in the wild, or at any
rate not domesticated.

For the few remaining days it still lacks meaning
in any practical order of the world, let us profit
from its virtues.[22]

What in fact are these 'practical' meanings but the
reflection on to things of that social order Ponge detests?
Gravel refers us on to the grass of the lawn, the lawn to
the villa, and the villa to the town and here we have,
once again, 'All these crude lorries that move *within us*,
these factories, workshops, theatres and public monu-
ments that make up *much more* than the backdrop to
our lives.'[23]

There is, then, first in Ponge a rejection of collusion.
He finds *within himself* words that are soiled and 'ready-
made' and *outside himself* objects that are domesticated
and abased. He will attempt in one and the same movement to de-humanize words by seeking out their 'semantic density' beneath their surface meaning and to
de-humanize things by scratching away their veneer of
utilitarian meanings. This means that one has to come at
the thing when one has eliminated within oneself what
Bataille calls the *project*. And this attempt depends on a
philosophical assumption which I shall confine myself, for

22 Ponge, 'The Pebble', in *The Nature of Things*, p. 65.
23 Ponge, 'Des raisons d'écrire', in *Le Parti pris des choses*, p. 162.

the moment, to revealing: in the Heideggerian world, the existent is, first, *Zeug* or item of equipment. To see it as *das Ding*, the temporo-spatial *thing*, the proper course is to 'neutralize' oneself. One stops, forms the project of suspending any project, and then remains in the attitude of '*nur verweilen bei*' (merely tarrying with). It is at this point that the thing emerges, being, all in all, merely a secondary aspect of the item of equipment—an aspect grounded in the last resort in equipmentality [*das Zeughafte*]—and Nature appears as a collection of inert things. Ponge's movement is the opposite: it is the thing that exists first for him in its inhuman solitude; man is the thing that transforms things into instruments. One merely has, then, to muzzle this social, practical voice inside oneself for the thing to disclose itself in its eternal, instantaneous truth. Ponge reveals himself here an anti-pragmatist, because he rejects the idea that, by his action, man confers its meaning upon the real in an *a priori* fashion. His primal intuition is of a *given* universe. He writes,

> I must first confess to an absolutely charming, longstanding, characteristic temptation that my mind finds irresistible:
>
> It is to assign to the world, to the set of things I see or imagine seeing not—as most philosophers do and *as is, no doubt, reasonable*[24] —the shape of a large sphere, a big, soft, nebulous and, as it were, misty pearl or, conversely a

---

24 My emphasis. [J.-P. S.]

limpid, crystalline one, in which the centre would, as one of them once said, be everywhere and the circumference nowhere . . . but rather, arbitrarily and by turns, the shape of the most peculiar, most asymmetrical, reputedly contingent things—and not just the shape, but all the characteristics . . . such as, for example, a lilac branch or a prawn.[25]

If he loves each flower and animal enough to give its shape and being to the universe by turns, then at least the existence of that universe is in no doubt for him; he at least considers it 'reasonable' to conceive it in the terms that dogmatic realism has lent it for twenty centuries. And in this solid universe, whether it be lilac, prawn or sphere of mist, man finds himself a thing among other things. In this almost naive conception, let us find, then, the affirmation of scientific materialism: that the object is preeminent over the subject. Being pre-exists knowing; Ponge's initial postulate is the same as the initial postulate of science. Like many artists and writers of his generation, Ponge began with methodical doubt; but he refused to challenge science. Perhaps this omission will come back to haunt him later.

But for the moment we have discovered our object. It is, in the end, the universe, with man in it. 'I would like to write a kind of *De rerum natura*. You can see the

---

25 Ponge, 'La forme du monde', in *Le Parti pris des choses*, p. 115.

difference from contemporary poets: it isn't *poems* I would like to write, but one single cosmogony.'

Why does this cosmogony present itself today in discontinuous fragments? This is because you have to build up an alphabet:

> The wealth of propositions contained in the slightest object is so great that I cannot yet conceive of anything but the simplest: a stone, a blade of grass, fire, a piece of wood, a piece of meat.[26]

So, for the moment, it isn't so much a question of writing a Cosmogony as of producing a kind of Compendium of Characteristics by the designation of elementary entities that can be combined to reproduce more complicated existents. There is, then, in Ponge's eyes, an absolute simplicity and an absolute complication; the idea doesn't cross his mind that everything is perfectly simple or infinitely complicated depending on the standpoint one adopts. A man lighting a cigarette is a perfectly simple thing, provided, however, that I regard this man with his cigarette as a single, signifying totality—that is to say, provided that I register the emergence of a *Gestalt*. But if I am wilfully blind to this synthetic form, then here I am with so much meat, bones and nerves on my hands, and amongst all this butcher's meat, I shall have to choose relatively simple 'pieces' susceptible

---

26 Ponge, 'Introduction au galet', in *Le Parti pris des choses*, p. 175.

of description. This is what Ponge does. But my question to him is: why does he grant the unity that he denies to the smoker to his femur or his biceps? We shall come back to this point later.

So here we are, then, in the countryside. The countryside has insinuated itself even into the city centre. A cabbage in a garden, a pebble on the strand, a lorry on the square, a cigarette in the ashtray or stuck in a mouth—these are all the same, because we have stripped out the *project*. Things are there, waiting for us. And what we notice first is that they call out for expression: 'the mute insistence [things] make that we speak them, as they deserve and for themselves—outside their usual meaning-value—without choice and yet in measured tones. But what a measure: their own.'[27]

We have to take this passage literally. This isn't a poet's formula for characterizing the calls that the most obscure, most deeply buried of our memories make to us. It is a direct intuition of Ponge's, as untheoretical as possible. He comes back to it insistently in *Le Parti pris des choses*, particularly in the admirable pages he devotes to vegetation.

[T]rees . . . let fly with their words, a flood of them, an eruption of green. They try to achieve a complete leafing out of words . . . They fling out words at random, or so they believe, fling out

---

27 Ponge, 'Les façons du regard', in *Le Parti pris des choses*, p. 120.

twigs on which to hang still more words . . .
Believing they can say everything, blanket the
whole world with a full range of words, they say
only 'trees' . . . Ever the same leaf, ever the same
way of unfolding, the same limits, forever identical leaves hung identically! . . . Ultimately,
nothing could stop them but this sudden observation: 'There's no getting away from trees by
way of trees.'[28]

He explains this further on in the following terms:

They are nothing but a will to express. Holding
nothing back for themselves, they cannot keep
one idea secret, they lay themselves completely
open, candidly, without reservation . . . [A]ll
drive to express themselves is unavailing, except
toward developing their bodies, as though for
us each desire required us thereafter to nourish
and sustain an additional limb. An infernal
increase of substance prompted by every idea![29]

I don't believe anyone has gone further in grasping
the being of things. Materialism and idealism aren't the
issue here. We are a very long way from theories; we are
at the heart of things themselves; and we see them suddenly like thoughts fleshed out by their own objects. As
though this idea that had set out to become the idea of

---

28 Ponge, 'The Cycle of Seasons', in *The Nature of Things*, p. 25.
29 Ponge, 'Fauna and Flora', in *The Nature of Things*, pp. 51–3.

a chair suddenly solidified from one end to the other and *became* chair. If we look at Nature *from the standpoint of the Idea*, we cannot escape this obsession with the absence of distinction between the possible and the real, which we find to a lesser degree in dreams and which is characteristic of Being-in-itself. The assertion is, in fact, always an assertion *of* something; in other words, the act of asserting is distinct from the thing asserted. But if we suppose the existence of an assertion in which what is asserted fills up the asserter and merges with him, then this assertion can no longer be asserted, for reasons of excessive plenitude and the immediate inherence of the container in the content. In this way, the entity is opaque to itself precisely because it is filled with itself. If it wishes to take a reflexive view of itself, then that view—leaf or branch—itself grows dense: it is a *thing*. This is the aspect of Nature we apprehend when we view it in silence: it is a petrified language. Hence the duty Ponge feels towards it: to make it manifest. For it is just this that is at issue: making something manifest. But Ponge's efforts differ profoundly from Gidean 'manifestation'. In 'making manifest', Gide is aiming to stitch Nature back together, to tighten its weft and at last make it exist on the plane of aesthetic perfection, so as to verify Wilde's paradoxical statement that 'nature imitates art.' Gidean 'manifestation' stands in the same relation to its object as the geometrical circle does to the 'rings' found in Nature. Ponge merely wants to lend his language to all these bogged-down, clogged-up words emerging all around him from earth, air and water. How can he do this? First he must go back to that naive attitude dear to all philosophical radicalisms—to Descartes, Bergson and Husserl: 'Let me pretend that I know nothing.'

> I look over the current state of the sciences: whole libraries on every part of each one of them . . . Should I begin, then, by reading and learning them? Several lifetimes would not suffice. Amid the enormous extent and quantity of knowledge acquired by each science, we are lost. The best option, then, is to regard everything as unknown and to stroll or recline in the woods or on the grass and start everything over again from the beginning.[30]

In this way Ponge is unwittingly applying the axiom at the origin of all Phenomenology: 'To the things themselves.'[31] His method will be love, a love that involves neither desire, fervour nor passion, but is total approval and total respect, 'extreme diligence in not troubling the object', such a perfect and detailed adaptation 'that your words forever treat everyone as this object treats them by the place it occupies, by what it resembles and by its qualities . . .' In short, it isn't so much about observing the pebble as settling into its heart and seeing the world with its eyes, the way the novelist, to depict his protagonists,

---

30 Ponge, 'Introduction au galet', in *Le parti pris des choses*, p. 177.
31 'Aux choses mêmes', '*An die Sache selbst*'.

slips into their minds and describes people and things as they appear to those protagonists. This stance enables us to see why Ponge calls his work a cosmogony rather than a cosmology. Because it isn't a matter of *describing*. You will find very little in him of those brilliant snapshots by which a Virginia Woolf or a Colette exactly render the *appearance* of an object. He speaks of the cigarette without saying a word about the white paper that surrounds it, of the butterfly almost without mentioning the designs mottling its wings: he isn't concerned with *qualities* but with *being*. And the being of each thing seems to him a project, an effort at expression, at a *certain* expression of a certain nuance of dryness, stupor, generosity or stillness. To get inside this effort, beyond the phenomenal aspect of the thing, is to have reached into its being. Hence the following discourse on method:

> The entire secret of the contemplator's happiness lies in his refusal to regard the invasion of his personality by things *as an evil*. To avoid this veering off into mysticism, one must (1) be precisely, that is to say expressly, aware of each of the things one has made the object of one's contemplation; (2) change objects of contemplation quite often and, overall, retain a degree of moderation. But the most important thing for the contemplator's health is the *naming*, as he goes along, of all the qualities he discovers;

the qualities that 'carry him away' must not carry him further than their exact, measured expression.[32]

This brings us back, then, to naming, which is where we started. It now appears as the practice of a Hellenic virtue of moderation. And yet let us be clear: in Ponge's eyes, if man names, he doesn't do so merely to fix as a notion something that is always in danger of degenerating into *ekstasis*, but because, ultimately, everything begins and ends for him with words; in naming, he fulfils his duties as a man: 'The Word is God; there is only the Word; I am the Word.'[33]

Consequently, the bestowing of names assumes the status of a religious ceremony. First, because it corresponds to the moment of renewal; through this renewal, man, diluted into the thing, withdraws, gathers himself and reassumes his human function. Second—and foremost—because the thing, as we have seen, awaits being named with all the ardour of its aborted expressiveness. As a result, naming is a metaphysical act of absolute value; it is the solid, definitive union of man and thing, because the *raison d'être* of the thing is to require a name and the function of man is to speak in order to give it

---

32 Ponge, 'Introduction au galet', in *Le parti pris des choses*, pp. 175–6.

33 This is at variance with the most recent editions of Ponge, which have: 'The Word is God; I am the Word; there is only the Word.' See Francis Ponge, 'La dérive du sage', in *Le Parti pris des choses*, p. 139. [Trans.]

one. This is why Ponge can write of the 'modification of things by the word':[34]

> Into a . . . wave, into a shapeless ensemble that fills up its content, or at least espouses its form to a certain degree—through waiting or through an accommodation, a kind of attention that is of this same nature—may enter that which will effect its modification: the word.
>
> For the things of the spirit, the word might be said then to be their state of rigour, their way of holding steady outside of their containers. Once this has been made understood, one will have the time to study their specifiable qualities calmly, minutely and diligently, and the pleasure of doing so.
>
> The most remarkable thing, striking one immediately, is a kind of growth, a sort of increase in volume of the ice in relation to the wave, and the breaking, by the ice itself, of the container, a previously indispensable form.[35]

This means that, by the very act that gives the thing its name, the idea becomes thing and makes its entry into the field of objective spirit. Equally, it isn't just a question of naming but of *making a poem*. By this, Ponge means

---

34 Ponge, 'De la modification des choses par la parole', in *Le Parti pris des choses*, p. 122.

35 Ponge, 'De la modification des choses par la parole', in *Le Parti pris des choses*, pp. 122–3.

a work of a quite particular sort that strictly excludes lyricism: after the fumblings and approximations that yielded the nouns and adjectives to him that will match the thing, these have to be gathered into a synthetic totality and this has to be done in such a way that the very organization of the Word in this totality exactly renders the emergence of the thing into the world and its inner articulation. It is precisely this which he terms a poem. Doubtless it isn't entirely the thing itself, as we have seen, and it preserves something of the relationship with man: 'Otherwise, each poem would please each and every individual, would please all of them all the time, as the objects of the sensations themselves please us and strike us.' But 'at least, by a kneading, a primordial disrespect of words etc., one will have to give the impression of a new idiom that will produce the effect of surprise and novelty of the objects of sensation themselves.'

And this poem, precisely because of the profound unity of the words in it, because of its synthetic structure and the agglutination of all its parts, will not be a mere copy of the thing but the thing itself.

> The poet must never offer a thought but an object. That is to say that he must even make thought assume the stance of an object.
>
> The poem is an object of delight offered to man, made and put in place especially for him.[36]

---

36 Ponge, 'Natare piscem doces', in *Le Parti pris des choses*, p. 130.

We meet up here once again with that trend common to the literature and painting of the twentieth century, which sees a painting, for example, not so much as an—albeit free—translation of nature, but as a nature in and of itself. But we must understand this clearly. It is the form itself, in its opacity, that is a thing here. The content remains the deep movement of the thing named. However this may be, when the poem is finished, the unity of the world is restored. In a sense, everything is actually expression, since things tend of themselves towards the Word, in the same way as Aristotelian Nature tends towards God; everything is expression, self-expression or an attempt at expression; and naming, which is the most human of acts, is also man's communion with the universe. But, in another sense, everything is *a thing*, since poetic naming has itself turned into stone. In Ponge's world, it is as though a subtle materialization seized meanings themselves from behind; or, rather, as though things and thoughts congealed. Thus the universe, which is for a moment pierced by thought, closes up and encloses thingly thought within itself, together with the things that have been thought. All is full: the Word has embodied itself and 'there is only Word.'[37]

That moment of *ek-stasis* in which he installs himself, outside of himself, in the heart of the thing Ponge terms 'contemplation' and we have seen that love, as he

---

37 'Il n'y a que du Verbe.' Presumably an allusion to the phrase 'Il n'y a que le Verbe' (there is only the Word) cited above. [Trans.]

defines it, is itself rather Platonic, since it is not accompanied by true possession. Yet we should not imagine that this intuition falls foul of the criticism normally made of strictly contemplative attitudes. This is because it is of a very particular kind. First, I shall happily term it 'active contemplation', for, far from suspending all dealings with the object, it presupposes, on the contrary, that one will adapt to it by a range of efforts whose only limitation is that they mustn't be utilitarian. Ponge tells us, for example, that, in order to bring out the singular qualities of the washing boiler:

> It isn't sufficient to have sat on a chair and contemplated it on many an occasion.
>
> Complainingly, you have to have lifted it, filled with its load of filthy fabrics, to put it on the fire, to which you have, in a way, to drag it, and then you have to set it down just on the edging of the fireplace.
>
> You have to have stirred the wood into flames beneath it to get it going gradually; to have tested often the temperature of its—tepid or boiling—sides; then to have listened to the deep inner rustling and lifted the cover several times to check it is operating freely and evenly.
>
> And you have, finally, to have put your arms around its boiling form once again, to set it back on the ground.

Perhaps by then you will have discovered it.[38]

It goes without saying that when Ponge executes these various forms of hard labour, doubtless to help his wife or some female relative, he strips them—to the great detriment of the washing, perhaps—of all practical significance. He sees in them merely an opportunity to form a closer contact with the boiler, to appreciate its weight, to gauge its circumference with his arms, to warm himself through with its heat. With other objects, his dealings will be even more disinterested. He opens doors for the pleasure of opening them: '. . . The joy of grabbing one of those tall barriers to a room by the porcelain knob in its middle;[39] he scalps their moss from 'the old austere rocks'. And there is, admittedly, no one who hasn't opened a door, dragged a boiler on to the range, scraped away a layer of moss or plunged their arm into the sea. The essential question is to know what you put into these things.

But, above all, Ponge hasn't let go for a moment of his revolutionary bias. His contemplation is active because it dashes from things the social order that is reflected in them. It stands opposed to any vain escapism: 'Against any desire for escape set contemplation and its

---

38 Francis Ponge, 'La lessiveuse', in *Pièces* (Paris: Gallimard, 1962), p. 73.

39 Ponge, 'The Pleasures of a Door', in *The Nature of Things*, p. 23. 'Knob' here translates Ponge's 'noeud', which means 'knot' and hence suggests 'navel'. [Trans.]

resources. No use leaving: transfer oneself to things.'[40] Inasmuch as it is de-humanizing, his intuition contributes to closing the material world over our heads, leaving us lost, like things, within it; it is little short of pantheistic. Let us call it a pantheism brought to a timely halt. We see, then, that his intuition operates as much *against* as *with*. However, its ultimate goal is the substitution of a true human order for the social order it dismantles. The bias towards things [*parti pris des choses*] leads to the object-lesson. The fact is that 'millions of feelings, as different from the little catalogue of those currently experienced by the most sensitive of people, are still to be known and experienced.' And it is amid things that we discover them. The aim, then, is to lay hold of them and bring them about in ourselves:

> For my part, I'd like to say that I am something very different and, for example, apart from all the qualities I share with the rat, the lion and the net, I aspire to that of the diamond and I feel total solidarity . . . with both the sea and the cliff that it attacks and also with the pebble thereby created . . . without prejudice to all the qualities that I expect to become aware of and gain effective enjoyment from subsequently, through the contemplation and naming of extremely different objects.[41]

40 Ponge, 'Introduction au galet', in *Le Parti Pris des Choses*, p. 174.
41 Ponge, 'Introduction au galet', in *Le Parti Pris des Choses*, p. 174.

This may perhaps be thought to display a naive animism, incompatible with the materialism Ponge was just professing: but it is, in fact, the opposite. When Ponge wishes to benefit from sentiments he sees as being enclosed in the heart of objects—and wishes others to benefit from them—he isn't, in any sense, regarding things as little silent people, but rather seeing people deliberately as things. He doubtless attributes 'ways-of-behaving' to inanimate objects. But this is precisely because he remains entirely behaviouristic and doesn't believe our 'behaviours' to be, *a priori*, of a different nature from theirs. In every thing there is a material effort, a striving and a project that makes up its unity and permanence. But we are constituted no differently. In his view, our unity is the unity of our muscles, tendons and nerves and that physiological striving that keeps the whole together until we die. Far from there being a humanization of the pebble here, there is a dehumanization of man, reaching even as far as his feelings. And if my very feelings are things, are particular orders that impose themselves on my innards, can we not speak of the feelings of stones? If I can fuel my anger, can I not maintain in myself, at least as an affective pattern, a certain type of sober, lofty dessication that will, for example, be the mark of the pebble. It isn't yet time to attempt to determine whether Ponge is right or wrong and how he may be right—perhaps in spite of himself. We are merely setting out his doctrine. The fact remains that this attempt to conquer virgin territories for our sensibilities seems to him a highly moral task. In achieving it, he will thus not merely have done the work of a painter, but genuinely fulfilled his mission as a man, since, as he has it, the proper notion of man is 'the word and morality: humanism.'

So what has he done? And has he succeeded? The moment has at last come to examine his works. And since he himself regards them as objects, let us examine them *as things*, which is how he himself sees cigarettes or snails, teasing out their meaning and internal articulation with no regard for the stated intentions of their author. We shall see then whether their 'way-of-behaving' corresponds in every particular to the theories we have just outlined.

II

Ponge's poems present themselves as chamfered constructions, each facet of which is a paragraph. Through each facet, we see the total object. But from a different point of view each time. The organic unit is, therefore, the paragraph: it is sufficient unto itself. Seldom is any transition effected between paragraphs. They are separated by a certain density of void. We don't move from one facet to the next, but one has to rotate the entire construct to bring a new facet before our eyes. Neither Ponge nor the reader benefits from any acquired impetus; there is, each time, a new beginning. Thus, the inner structure of the poem is, manifestly, juxtaposition. It isn't possible, however, for memory to prevent itself from conserving the past paragraphs and bringing them to bear upon those I am currently reading. This is also because, through this mosaic, a single idea is developing. Often, as with *Le Mimosa*, the poem takes the form of a series of approximations and each approximation is a paragraph. *Le Mimosa* presents the aspect of a theme followed by variations: all motifs are indicated first—or almost all; and each paragraph presents itself as a fresh combination of these motifs with the introduction of very few new elements. Each of these variations is then rejected as imperfect, as transcended or buried by a new combination that starts again from scratch. Yet it remains there, if only as the image of what has already been done and is no longer to be done. And the final 'poem' will merge all these trial runs into a 'definitive version'. In this way, each paragraph is present, in spite of everything, to the next paragraph. But not in the style of that 'multiplicity of interpenetration' that Bergson speaks of,[42] nor like the elapsed notes of a melody that are still audible in the next note, colouring it and lending it its meaning: the past paragraph *haunts* the present one and seeks to merge into it. But it cannot: the other repels it with all its density.

The organic unit being the paragraph, each sentence takes on a differentiated function within that totality.

---

42 Henri Bergson, *Time and Free Will* (authorized translation from the French of *Essai sur les données immédiates de la conscience* by F. L. Pogson) (New York: Harper and Brothers, 1960), p. 75.

We can no longer speak here of juxtaposition: there is movement, transition, ascent, re-descent, slippage, vection, beginning and end. I read the first lines of 'Sea Shores': the initial sentence is an unconditioned assertion. The second, beginning with a 'but', corrects it. The third, opening with a 'This . . . is why' draws the conclusion from the first two, and the fourth, beginning with 'For' brings ultimate justification to the whole. Here, then, is movement and a highly developed division of labour—the very image of life; we are no longer dealing with a polypary, but with an evolved organism. Yet a kind of rather complex unease gives me pause. This bustling, teeming life has something suspicious about it. I open Pascal's *Pensées* at random:

> Let man then contemplate the whole of nature in its full and lofty majesty, let him avert his view from the lowly objects around him. Let him behold that brilliant light set like an eternal lamp to illuminate the universe, let the earth seem to him like a point in comparison with the vast orbit described by that star and let him be amazed that this vast orbit is itself but a very small point in comparison with the one described by the stars rolling around the firmament. But if our gaze stops here, let our imagination pass beyond; it will sooner tire of conceiving things than nature of producing them. This whole visible world is only an imperceptible trace in the ample bosom

of nature. No idea approaches it. However much we may inflate our conceptions, etc. . . .[43]

See how, in Pascal, the full stop represents a sigh, not a pause. It has been put between the first two sentences for considerations of breathing and visual pleasure rather than meaning, since, in both the first and the second sentence, we find similar exhortations separated by mere commas. The result is a flow that runs from one sentence to the next and a deep unity beneath these superficial divisions; and the second sentence benefits so greatly from the impetus imparted by the first that it doesn't even trouble to name its subject: it is the same 'man' who inhabits both. After this strong opening, the third sentence can catch its breath and vary slightly the mode of presentation of the same exhortation; the beginning was so violent that this sentence is playing on velvet; the mind puts it together, in spite of itself, with the two preceding ones. There is a move here now from exhortation to statement. But see what wariness there is: it is within the third sentence, after the frail barrier of a semi-colon, that this transition occurs. With the result that this central sentence is the pivot of the paragraph: in it the initial movement dies; in it this stirring of calm,

---

43 Blaise Pascal, *Pensées* (Roger Ariew ed. and trans.) (Indianapolis: Hackett Publishing Company, 2005), p. 58 (translation modified). For obvious reasons, I have restored Pascal's original French punctuation, but I have also reinserted Pascal's reference to the 'ample bosom' (*l'ample sein*) of nature, which Ariew renders merely as 'amplitude'. [Trans.] Ponge, 'Préface aux Sapates', in *Le Parti Pris des Choses*, p. 111.

concentric waves begins that will carry us to the end. Here is a genuine melodic unity. Melodic to the point of setting our teeth on edge somewhat.

By contrasting it with this, we can understand the structure of Ponge's paragraphs better: his sentences clearly beckon to each other, essay transitions, attempt to build bridges. But each is so dense, so definitive and its internal cohesion is such that, as we saw just now with his paragraphs, there are gaps and emptiness between them. The entire life of the poem lies between two full stops; and the full stops here assume their maximum value: that of a tiny annihilation of the world, which takes shape again a few moments later. Hence the disconcerting savour of the object: the sentences are constructed as a function of one another. With hooks and 'eyes'; they are hook-shaped and should be able to catch, but an imperceptible distance means the hooks fall off without grasping on to anything. The unity of the paragraph is set before us, but it is a semantic unity, too immaterial, too much a thing of intelligibility to be tasted. It is a ghostly unity, present everywhere, but nowhere tangible. And the 'Fors', the 'Buts' and the 'Howevers' take on an ambiguous, rather solemn dimension as a result, because they were made for connecting and for effecting transitions, and suddenly they are elevated to the dignity of first beginnings. At which they are as surprised as anyone (I might say if I wanted to ape Ponge's style).

There are, admittedly, many possible explanations for this aspect of *Le Parti pris des choses*. Ponge has warned us himself that he worked in a discontinuous fashion. He has a job that takes all his attention for ten hours a day. He writes in the evening and only for short periods. Each evening everything has to be begun again, without any existing momentum or springboard. Each evening he has to get back into the presence of things—and of paper. Each evening he has to discover a new facet and write a new paragraph. But he forewarns us himself against this excessively material explanation:

> Moreover, even if I had the time, it doesn't seem to me that I'd have the inclination to work at length, and several times, on the same subject. What counts for me is to seize almost every evening on a new object and derive pleasure and instruction from it.[44]

There is something like a bias towards the discontinuous here that amounts to an original choice. We ought per- haps to show—it wouldn't be difficult but would take us too far from our purpose—why the 'lovers of souls', like Barrès, are on the side of continuity and the 'lovers of things' prefer the discrete, as Renard and Ponge do. The important thing here for us is to define the effect— whether consciously obtained or not—of these discon- tinuities. It represents perhaps the most immediate

---

44 Ponge, 'Préface aux Sapates', in *Le Parti Pris des Choses*, p. 111.

attractions of Ponge's works—and one that is most difficult to explain. It seems to me that, in their relationship with each other, his sentences are like those solid bodies you see in the paintings of Braque and Juan Gris; between them the eye has to establish a hundred different unities, a thousand relations and correspondences, to make them eventually into a *single* picture; these objects are, however, ringed with lines so thick and dark and are so deeply centred on themselves, that the eye bounces perpetually from the continuous to the discontinuous, attempting to fuse together different splashes of the same violet and running up, at every turn, against the impenetrability of the mandolin and the water jug. But in Ponge's work this flitting about seems to me to have a very particular meaning: it constitutes the poem itself in its intuitive form as a perpetually evanescent synthesis of living unity and inorganic dispersion. Let us not forget that the poem is a *thing* here and that, as a thing, it claims a certain type of existence which the ordering of sentences and paragraphs necessarily confers upon it. Now, it seems to me this type of existence could be defined as that of an enchanted statue; we are dealing with marble figures haunted by life. These paragraphs perpetually visited by the memory of other paragraphs that are incapable of articulating themselves with them; these sentences which, in their inorganic solitude, are abuzz with calls to other sentences they cannot join— doesn't all this resemble an abortive effort on the part of stone to achieve organized existence? We find here an intuitive image, provided by the style and the writing, of the way Ponge wants us to envisage 'things'. We shall have to come back to this point.

Ponge's sentences, suspended as they are like this in the void by a subtle breakdown of the links between them, are enormously affirmative. The author's own taste is the first reason for this: he wants to leave 'proverbs' behind him. By proverbs, I mean sentences already petrified and laden with meaning, whose power of assertion is such that a whole society takes them as its own. We therefore understand this severe economy of words that he wants to achieve everywhere—that the conjunction 'and' has been practically eliminated from his work, for example, or appears in it only as a ceremonial exordium—and that subordinate clauses, weighted with this omnipresent affirmation, some-times stand up on their own, without any main clause, between two full stops, looking rather like preliminary provisions in a legal decree:

> But since each caterpillar head was left blinded and blackened, each torso emaciated by the veritable explosion which sent flaring up symmetrical wings,
>
> The erratic butterfly alights simply at the whim of its haphazard flight, or so it seems.[45]

But it is the primary function of the act of assertion, with all its pomp, to imitate the categorical bursting-forth of

---

45 Ponge, 'The Butterfly', in *The Nature of Things*, p. 32.

the thing. Let us not forget that it isn't Ponge's aim to describe the undulation of appearances, but the internal substance of the object at the precise point where that substance determines itself. His sentence consequently reproduces this generative movement. It is, first and foremost, genetic and synthetic. Ponge's problem connects here with Renard's: how is one to get the greatest possible number of ideas into a single sentence? But whereas Renard was pursuing the impossible ideal of silence, Ponge aims to reproduce the thing at a single stroke. The words have to crystallize as the eye moves over them and the sentence has, at the end, to have reproduced the emergence of something. But, since this emergence has the stubbornness of things, not the flexibility of life, since it isn't so much a birth as a kind of fixed apparition, then instead of being propagated softly from sentence to sentence like a wave, the generative movement has to dash against the buffer of the full stop and stop dead in its tracks. Hence the frequent sentence structure of a rapid, liquid world of appositions at the beginning, followed suddenly by a halt in the form of a short, pithy main clause: the thing 'has congealed' and is suddenly bounded. Here, for example, is the butterfly: 'Miniature sailboat of the skies, ill-treated by the winds as a petal superfluity, footloose it goes breezing about the garden.'[46]

Ponge's sentence is, in itself, a world articulated in minute detail, where the place of every word is calculated,

---

46 Ponge, 'The Butterfly', in *The Nature of Things*, p. 32.

where it is the function of enjambments and inversions to present the facts in their true order, but also to figure as a distant memory of symbolism and the syntactic inventions of Mallarmé. Sometimes, in this world in fusion, there are sudden solidifications, the formation of lumps—mostly of adverbs—and then entire members of sentences bulking large as sticky masses and manifesting a kind of independence. This is because Ponge feels compelled hurriedly to describe, within his sentences themselves, the elements that make up the 'thing' being studied and their genesis. And so there are things within the thing and geneses within the genesis. This is the rain:

> Moulding to *the entire surface of a small tin roof that's visible below*
> it trickles in a thin skim moiréd *in eddies from the imperceptible bumps and ripples of the metal sheet.*
> In the adjoining gutter
> it sluices along *with all the application of a shallow rivulet gently pitched*
> then plunges abruptly
> *an absolutely vertical strand rather loosely tressed*
> straight to the ground where it shatters
> and dashes up *in glittering bead-tipped needles.*[47]

---

47 Ponge, 'Rain', in *The Nature of Things*, p. 13. I have italicized the phrases that stand in isolation. Note the mimetic nature of the sentence that actually ends at 'shatters' and bounces up again weakly like rain.

There remain the words, whose 'semantic density' has to convey the richness of things. This is, in fact, the least striking aspect. We undoubtedly find a happy levity towards language in Ponge's work, a certain way of manhandling it, of making puns, of inventing, where need be, words like 'gloriolous' or 'floribund', but in him this is more like a smile of deliverance. 'As an ex-martyr of language, you'll grant me the right not to take it seriously every day.'[48] And doubtless too he lingers more than anyone else over the correspondences between words and the things to which they refer: '. . . what makes my work so difficult is that the name of the mimosa is already perfect. Knowing both the plant and the name of the mimosa, it becomes difficult to find a better word to define the thing than the name itself.'[49]

But what counts, above all, is a sensual affection for names, a way of squeezing them to make them yield up all their meaning. Take, for example, 'it goes breezing about the garden,' which has its full impact only if we juxtapose the idea of wandering over undefined areas contained in the word 'breezing' with the confined, carefully polished, perfect quality in the word 'garden'. In this regard, Ponge should be read attentively, word by word; and re-read. There is profundity in his choice of words and it is this profundity that dictates the cascading

---

48 Ponge, 'Le mimosa', in *La rage de l'expression*, p. 80.
49 Ponge, 'Le mimosa', in *La rage de l'expression*, p. 80.

rhythm in which they should be read. But seldom are they chosen with that concerted impropriety he initially had in mind. And, though we must first register that his desire to produce thing-poems has been almost entirely fulfilled, we should also acknowledge that he failed in his attempt to give, 'the impression—by a kneading of words and a primordial disrespect for them—of a new idiom that will produce the effect of surprise and novelty made by the sensory objects themselves.'

It is time to move on now to examine content. But not without having noted that these sentences that are so sturdy and could easily veer towards solemnity are lightened and, as it were, hollowed out by a kind of innocent playfulness that gets everywhere. Eventually Ponge himself steps from the shadows and speaks about himself. Not as the character he normally affects to be, whom I imagine to be more sombre, but as a kind of ironic, gossipy, naive entomologist, reminiscent of one of Fabre's charming caricatures. This is because he conceives his poems in a happy state, when he is at his best. They are no doubt, as we have seen, revolutionary acts. But in the act itself he finds his deliverance and his pleasure:

> One ought to be able to give this title to all poems: Reasons to live happily. At least where I am concerned, those that I write are each like the note I try to take when a moment of meditation or contemplation lights the fuse within

my body of a few words that give it new vigour
and persuade it to live a few more days.[50]

* * *

As we have seen, Ponge doesn't observe or describe. He
neither seeks after nor captures the qualities of the object.
Nor do things seem to him, as they do to Kant, a pole X,
something on which to hang sensory qualities. Things
have *meanings*. Everything must be subordinated to
grasping and establishing these meanings, these 'reasons
in the raw or natural state when they have just been discovered amid the unique circumstances that surround
them at that same second'.[51] Reasons, meanings, ways-
of-behaving: it is all the same. Yet it needs a special kind
of lighting to see them. This is why the angle of approach
varies from object to object. The mimosa is seen from the
front, at the point when its yellow balls, its 'gloriolous
chicks' 'cheep with gold', whilst its palms are already
giving out signs of discouragement. With the shrimp, by
contrast, we are going to try to catch it at the moment
when 'a translucence as effective as the creature's darting
motions ultimately removes, even when seen immobile,
all semblance of continuity from its presence.'[52] The

---

50 Ponge, 'Raisons de vivre heureux', in *Le Parti pris des choses*, p. 166.

51 Ponge, 'Raisons de vivre heureux', in *Le Parti pris des choses*, p.
166. Ponge's 1948 text of this poem has 'reason' in the singular. Sartre
may be referring to an earlier version (Ponge dates the original poem
'1928–29'). [Trans.]

52 Ponge, 'The Shrimp', in *The Nature of Things*, pp. 56–7.

books teach that the butterfly is born from the caterpillar. Yet it isn't at the point of its metamorphosis that we shall look for it, but in the garden, when it seems suddenly to arise in droves, newborn from the earth: this is its true genesis. The pebble, on the other hand, demands to be understood on the basis of the rocks and the sea that give birth to it: we shall come to it after a long preamble on stones.

Concerned to allow every thing its real dimensions—rather than the dimensions it assumes in our eyes, which depends on our measurement—we shall see the sea shell on the beach as an object 'out of all proportion' or as an 'enormous monument'.[53] And it will seem to us then that we are viewing some Dalí painting in which a giant oyster, capable of gobbling up three men at a single go, is lying on an infinitely monotonous stretch of white sand.

In appearance, then, we are exemplarily docile, and it is our aim merely to grasp the dialectic of the object and submit ourselves to it. And, with each reality that comes before us, we shall try to 'leav[e] it to enter on its own the coils of circumlocution . . . and ultimately to grasp through words at the dialectic point dictated by its form and environment, its mute condition, and the pursuit of its own true profession.'[54]

---

53 Ponge, 'Notes for a Sea Shell', in *The Nature of Things*, p. 46.
54 Ponge, 'The Shrimp', in *The Nature of Things*, p. 56.

Yet is this how Ponge really proceeds? Does the impression that his poems leave us match his declared method? Didn't he come to things with preconceived ideas? We must examine this closely.

I note first that a large part of the charming mystery surrounding Ponge's productions derives from the fact that there is constant mention of man's relationships with the thing in question, but these are stripped of all human meaning. Let us take the oyster:

> It is a world categorically closed in upon itself. And yet it can be opened: that takes gripping it in a folded rag, plying a nicked and dull-edged knife, chipping away at it over and over. Probing fingers get cut on it, nails get broken. It's a rough job.[55]

This is a universe peopled by human beings and yet bereft of them. Which is the more oyster, the oyster itself or that strange, stubborn indeterminate being, who seems to come straight from a Kafka novel, torturing it with a 'nicked' knife, without our being able to guess the reasons for such zeal, given that we haven't been told that the oyster is edible? And now this being itself—half-divinity and half-violent outburst that it is—disappears and gives way to these probing fingers that are not unlike those of the rapping hands in Fra Angelico's frescoes. A strange world, in which man is present through his

---

55 Ponge, 'The Oyster', in *The Nature of Things*, p. 22.

undertakings, but absent as spirit or project. A closed world, that one can neither enter nor leave, but which calls most specifically for a human witness: for the writer of *Le Parti pris des choses* and its reader. The inhumanity of things throws me back on myself; in this way, consciousness, extricating itself from the object, finds itself in the Hegelian dialectic. Yet consciousness, in Ponge's view, is itself a thing.

Where does the unity of the object derive from? This is Ponge's pebble:

> . . . smaller day by day but ever certain of its form, blind, secure, and dry within, by nature it would sooner be reduced by the seas than blended in. So when stone, vanquished, is turned at last to sand, water still can't penetrate as it does with dust.[56]

I see Ponge as affirming here—*against science*—the unity of the stone that offers itself as such to his perception. But when he extends this unity as far as the scattered fragments of the pebble, as far as that pebble dust, I would argue that he is relying neither on science nor on sensory intuition, but solely on his human capacity for unification. For perception certainly provides him with the unity of the pebble, but not the unity of pebble and sand. And science definitely teaches him that sand comes, largely, from broken pebbles; but it adds that—

---

56 Ponge, 'The Pebble', in *The Nature of Things*, p. 67.

Nature being exteriority—there never was any unity in stones, but simply a collection of molecules obeying various different types of motion. Judgement and decision are needed to carry over on to these metamorphoses, which geology reconstitutes, the unity that perception vouchsafes to us. Yet man is absent; the object precedes —and crushes—the subject. The unity of the pebble comes from the pebble itself and imparts itself to its tiniest particles—to that stone in smithereens—by way of an inner force that corresponds to its original project and must probably be termed *magical*. The cigarette, the orange, bread, fire and meat can all be seen in this same light. All these entities have a cohesion that is carefully distinct from life, which nonetheless accompanies them through all their various transformations. This is a curious frozen spontaneity, bearing some similarity with the intentness on its part that maintains the circle as a circle, when, from another standpoint, it breaks down perpetually into an infinity of juxtaposed points: these objects are bewitched.

Let us get closer to them. I can no longer distinguish now between the gymnast—that *man* Ponge was describing a moment ago—and the crate or cigarette he is describing now. The fact is that he downgrades the one while elevating the status of the others. We have seen that he reduced the *acts* of this athlete to being the mere *properties* of a species. But, conversely, he endows inanimate things with specific properties. Of the gymnast, he says: 'To top it off, he sometimes plummets from the rigging like a caterpillar, only to bounce back on his feet.'[57] And of the cigarette: '. . . the atmosphere, hazy yet dry, wispy, with the cigarette always placed right in the thick of it, once engaged in its continuous creation'.[58] Or of water: '. . . water endlessly ravels in upon itself, constantly refuses to assume any form, tends only to self-humiliation, prostrating itself, all but a corpse.'[59] This isn't about the states into which an external cause (for example, gravity) has put the thing, but about the shared habits of a species, and this assumes that each object is to some degree independent of its environment and attributes a specific internal necessity to it. The outcome is that this 'Cosmogony' takes on the features of a natural history. In the end, human beings, animals, plants and minerals are all put on an equal footing. It isn't that all entities have been raised—or lowered—to the pure form of life, but the same close cohesion has been bestowed upon each by—to use Hegelian language—projecting interiority on to exteriority. What gives the things in Ponge's lapidary their ambiguous originality is the fact that they are not *animate*. They retain their inertia, their fragmentation, their 'stupefaction', that perpetual tendency to collapse that Leibniz called their stupidity. Ponge does more than merely maintain these

57 Ponge, 'The Gymnast', in *The Nature of Things*, p. 39.

58 Ponge, 'The Cigarette', in *The Nature of Things*, p. 20.

59 Ponge, 'Water', in *The Nature of Things*, p. 37.

qualities; he proclaims them. But they are gathered together and linked up by 'properties' or even feelings that metamorphose as they touch them and, imparting to them a little of their inner tension, both are petrified and disintegrate at one and the same time. Look at the stone, it is alive. Look at life, it is stone. Anthropomorphic comparisons abound, at the same time as they cast a—relatively dubious—light on things, their effect is mainly to abase the human, to 'tangle it up', as our author has it. Let's take another look at water:

> Water is colourless and glistening, formless and cool, passive and determined in its single vice: gravity. With exceptional means at its disposal to gratify the vice: circumvention, perforation, infiltration, erosion.[60]

Isn't this like a description of a family of plants? But Ponge goes on:

> The vice plays an inner role as well: water endlessly ravels in upon itself, constantly refuses to assume any form, tends only to self-humiliation, prostrating itself, all but a corpse.[61]

This inner collapse brings us back abruptly to the inorganic. The unity of water vanishes almost entirely. We hesitate to go down a path that would lead us to one of those fantastical limp, boneless characters of folk tale,

60 Ponge, 'Water', in *The Nature of Things*, p. 37.
61 Ponge, 'Water', in *The Nature of Things*, p. 37.

who are always ready to fall flat and whom one lifts by an ear, but who immediately throw themselves flat on their faces again; or to take that other path that shows us all the particles of water coming unstuck, its very essence being pulverized, affirming against any attempt at unification the omnipotence of inertia and passivity. And just as we are at the crossroads, in that state of indecision the Ponge reader never escapes, the poet suddenly adds: 'You might almost say that water is insane.'[62] Who cannot see that in this passage it isn't water having a new character attributed to it, but madness which undergoes a secret metamorphosis, which *transforms into water* because it has touched its surface, which becomes, both within and outside man, an inorganic behaviour? I contend the same of all the passions Ponge bestows upon his things. They are so many meanings that he takes from man, so many techniques to maintain this subtle state of disequilibrium he wants to put us into.

What are the relations between the object thus described and its environment? They cannot be relations of pure exteriority. Very often, what belongs to the external world and settles on the object for a moment is incorporated into the object by Ponge and made one of its properties: it is the pebble that 'dissipates' the sea water that flows over it, not the sun; gravity is a 'vice' of water, not an external demand upon it. This, we may say, is what happens with observation: I see a gas-filled

62 Ponge, 'Water', in *The Nature of Things*, p. 37.

balloon rising and I speak of its 'uplift' or I say, with Aristotle, that its natural place is on high. What could be more natural for Ponge, since he has decided to show things as he sees them?

Indeed he has. And this would be perfect if he refrained, as he promised to do, from any recourse to science. But we see that, by a deliberate new ambiguity, Ponge has made this universe of pure observation *also* and *at the same time* a universe of science. It is his scientific knowledge that constantly lights his way and guides him, enabling him to question his object the more precisely. Leaves are 'taken aback by slow oxidation',[63] plants 'exhale carbon dioxide by the chlorophyll function, like a sigh lasting night after night.'[64] In writing of the pebble, Ponge describes the birth and cooling of the earth, doing so magnificently in fact. His images are, at times, merely metaphors intended to give more agreeable expression to a scientific law. He writes, for example, that the sun 'forces water into a perpetual cycle, treating it like a caged squirrel on its wheel'.[65] The magical universe of observation enables us to glimpse—from beneath— the world of science and its determinism:

---

63 Ponge, 'Trees coming undone within a sphere of fog'—'Water', in *The Nature of Things*, p. 23.

64 Ponge, 'Faune et flore', in *Le Parti pris des choses*, p. 85. In *The Nature of Things*, Fahnestock is working here from a different edition of the text. [Trans.]

65 Ponge, 'Water', in *The Nature of Things*, p. 38.

To the mind casting about for ideas which has first been nourished on images such as these, nature in respect to stone will ultimately seem, too simplistically perhaps, like a clock whose mechanism is made up of cogwheels revolving at very different rates, though driven by a single motor.[66]

And this mechanistic vision is so strong in him that it causes in his book a kind of disappearance of liquidity. Water is defined by its collapse, rain is compared to a 'rather loosely tressed . . . strand', to peas, marbles and needles; it is explained by a 'mechanism . . . like clock-work'.[67] The sea is, at times, a 'pseudo-organic accumulation of veils strewn evenly across three quarters of the globe' and, at times, a 'voluminous marine tome' riffled and turned down at the corners by the wind.[68] These transmutations of elements are, admittedly, the province of poet and painter; it was such effects that Proust admired in Elstir.[69] But Elstir also transmuted the earth into water. Here we feel that things have a *solid* base. 'LIQUID is what seeks to obey gravity rather than maintain its form, forgoes all form to obey its gravity.'[70] We

---

66 Ponge, 'The Pebble', in *The Nature of Things*, p. 64.

67 Ponge, 'Rain', in *The Nature of Things*, p. 13.

68 Ponge, 'Sea Shores', in *The Nature of Things*, p. 36, p. 33.

69 Elstir is a fictional impressionist painter in Proust's *A la recherche du temps perdu*. [Trans.]

70 Ponge, 'Water', in *The Nature of Things*, p. 37.

notice, then, that liquidity is a function of matter—and that *there is*, ultimately, a matter. It is this perpetual flitting from interiority to exteriority that gives Ponge's poems their originality and power; it is these little collapses within a single object that reveal *states* beneath its *properties*, and then it is the sudden recoveries that all at once unify states into *behaviours* and even feelings; it is this disposition of mind he awakens in the reader, this sense of never feeling at rest anywhere, of doubting whether matter isn't animated and if the soul's stirrings aren't quakings of matter; it is these perpetual exchanges that make him show man as the little bit of meat around a few bones and, conversely, meat as a 'sort of factory . . . Tubing, blast furnaces, vats, traffic with trip hammers, grease tubs',[71] this way of unifying the mechanical systems of science with the formulas of magic and, suddenly, of showing the universal determinism beneath the magic. In the end, the solid predominates. The solid and science, which has the last word.

Ponge has, in this way, written some admirable poems that are entirely original in tone, and created a material nature all his own. We can ask no more of him. We must add that his project is, by the ideas behind it, one of the most curious and perhaps one of the most important of our day. But if we want to bring out its importance, we have to prevail upon its author to throw over certain contradictions that mask and mar it.

71 Ponge, 'The Cut of Meat', in *The Nature of Things*, p. 39.

First, he hasn't been faithful to his original intention: he came to things not, as he claimed, with naive wonderment, but with a materialist bias. In fact, with Ponge it isn't so much a question of having a preconceived philosophical system as of having made an original choice of his selfhood. For his work is aimed as much at expressing this as at rendering the objects on which he is focussing. That choice is quite difficult to define. Rimbaud said:

If I have any taste, it is hardly for anything but earth and stones.[72]

And he dreamed of enormous massacres that would deliver the earth of its populations, fauna and flora. Ponge isn't so bloodthirsty. He's a 'vanilla' Rimbaud. And *Le Parti pris des choses* might well be called 'geology without massacres'. He even seems, on the face of it, to love flowers, animals and even people. And no doubt he does so. A great deal. But on condition that they are first petrified. He has a passion, a vice, for the inanimate, material *thing*. For the solid. Everything is solid in his work: from his sentences to the deepest foundations of his universe. If he ascribes human behaviour to mineral objects, it is in order to mineralize human beings. If he borrows ways of being from things, it is in order to mineralize himself. Perhaps we are justified in glimpsing a great necrological dream behind his revolutionary undertaking: the dream of enwrapping everything living—and man in particular—

---

72 Rimbaud, *A Season in Hell*, p. 41.

in the shroud of matter. Everything that comes from his hands is a *thing*, including, most especially, his poems. And his ultimate desire is that this whole civilization, together with his books, should one day appear as an immense necropolis of seashells to some higher ape, itself a thing, that will leaf abstractedly through these remnants of our glory. He has a premonition of this ape's gaze; he can already sense it upon himself: beneath these petrifying eyes, he feels his humours solidifying, he is turning into a statue; it is all over, he is one with the rock and the pebble, the stupefaction of stone paralyses his arms and legs. It is for this inoffensive, radical catastrophe that his writings aim to prepare. For this disaster that he needs the services of science and a materialist philosophy. And I see this first as a way of eliminating at a stroke all the sources of his suffering—the abuse, the injustice, the rotten disorder of the society into which he has been cast. But, even more than this, it seems he has opted for a quick path to symbolically fulfilling our shared desire *to exist after the manner of the 'in-itself'*. What fascinates him in the thing is its mode of existence, its total adherence to self, its stillness. Anxious flight, anger and anguish are banished in the insensible imperturbability of the pebble. I have observed elsewhere that the desire of all of us is to exist *with complete consciousness* in the mode of being of things: to be entirely a consciousness and, at the same time, entirely a stone. Materialism provides a theoretical satisfaction of this dream since it tells human beings they are merely mechanisms. I thus have the dismal pleasure of *feeling* myself think and *knowing* myself to be a material system. Ponge, it seems to me, isn't content with this pure theoretical knowledge; he it is who has made the most radical effort to have this purely theoretical knowledge descend into intuition. If he were to be able to unite the two, he would in fact have done the trick. And this flitting between interiority and exteriority which I mentioned a moment ago has a precise function: for want of a *real* fusion between consciousness and thing, Ponge has us oscillate between the two at very great velocity, hoping to achieve fusion at the upper limit of the oscillation.

But this isn't possible. He can have us flit between the two as quickly as he likes, but it is always *he* who is sending us from the one extreme to the other. He may close the world over himself with all that is in it, but he still ends up on the outside, staring in at things, all alone. We have already encountered this effort to see oneself through the eyes of an alien species, to rest from the painful duty of being a subject; we have seen it a hundred times, in different forms, in Bataille, Blanchot and the Surrealists. It represents the meaning of modern fantastic literature and also that of the highly individual materialism of our author.[73] On each occasion it has come to nothing. This is because the person making the effort, by the very fact of making it, becomes lost to himself

---

73 It is one of the consequences of the Death of God. So long as God lived, man was at ease: he knew he was being looked at. Today, when man is the only God and it is beneath his gaze that everything flourishes, he twists his neck round to try to see himself.

and projects himself to a point beyond where his strivings were located. Like Hegel, not being able, whatever he does, to get inside Hegelianism. Ponge's endeavour is doomed to failure like all others of the same kind.

And yet it has had an unexpected outcome. Ponge has locked up everything in the world, including himself insofar as he is a thing; all that remains is his contemplative consciousness which, precisely because it is consciousness *of* the world, finds itself necessarily *outside of* the world: a naked, almost impersonal consciousness. What has he done but effect the 'phenomenological reduction'? And doesn't this consist, in fact, in 'bracketing out' the world in order to rid oneself of all preconceived ideas? The world is no longer representation or transcendent reality then. Neither matter nor spirit. It is simply there—and I am conscious of it. What an excellent starting point, if Ponge were to accept it, for approaching 'things themselves' without the slightest prejudice! Science would be in the world, but bracketed out. Ponge would only have to say truly what he saw—and we know how powerfully he sees. Nothing would be lost—except perhaps this bias towards treating human beings as stuffed dummies. For they would have to be accepted with their human meanings, instead of setting out from a theoretical materialism forcibly to reduce them to the status of automatons. This slight change would be no bad thing, since Ponge's *only* bad writings—and they are very bad—are 'R. C. Seine No.' and 'Le restaurant Lemeunier', which are about human communities.[74] The *meaning* of things and their 'ways-of-behaving' would shine out all the more brightly, for, in the end, in Ponge's strange materialism, if everything may be said to be matter, on the other hand, everything is thought, since everything is expression. We have to continue to agree with him that things can teach us ways of being: I want him to be a lion, a pebble, a rat, a sea, and I want to be one with him. I shall refuse to believe, just as he does, that it is our psychological experience that enables physical matter to be shaped symbolically. But shall I conclude, as he does, that the object precedes the subject here? That isn't necessary. I have written elsewhere, if I may be permitted to quote myself:

> The slimy does not symbolize any psychic atti-
> tude *a priori*; it manifests a certain relation of
> being with itself and this relation has originally
> a psychic quality because I have discovered it in
> a plan of appropriation and because the slimi-
> ness has returned my image to me. Thus I am
> enriched from my first contact with the slimy,
> by an ontological pattern that is valid, beyond
> the distinction between psychic and non-psy-
> chic, for interpreting the ontological meaning
> of all the existents of a certain category, this cat-
> egory arising, moreover, like an empty skeletal
> framework *before* the experience with different

---

74 Ponge, The Nature of Things, pp. 41–5.

kinds of sliminess. I have projected it into the world by my original project when faced with the slimy; it is an objective structure of the world . . . What we say concerning the slimy is valid for all the objects which surround the child. The simple revelation of their matter extends his horizon to the extreme limits of being and thereby bestows upon him a collection of *clues* for deciphering the being of all human facts.[75]

Given this, I don't, however, think that 'by transferring ourselves to things', as Ponge wants us to do we find in them previously unknown ways of feeling, nor that we have then to borrow these from things in order to enrich ourselves with them. What we find everywhere—in the inkwell, on the phonograph needle or on the honey on a sandwich—is ourselves, always ourselves. And this range of indistinct, obscure feelings that we bring into being are something we had already—or, rather, we *were* those feelings. Only they couldn't be seen, they were hidden in the bushes, between stones, almost uselessly. For man isn't rolled up inside himself, but is outside, always outside, between earth and sky. The pebble has an interior, man

75 Jean-Paul Sartre, *Being and Nothingness* (Hazel E. Barnes trans.) (London: Methuen and Co Ltd, 1976), pp. 611–12, translation modified (Barnes renders '*le sens d'être de tous les existants d'une certaine catégorie*' as 'the meaning *of being and of* all the existents of a certain category' [p. 611, my emphasis], which clearly cannot be correct). [Trans.]

does not: but he does lose himself so that the pebble may exist. And all these 'rotten' human beings Ponge wants to get away from or be rid of are also 'rats, lions, nets and diamonds'. They are so, precisely because they 'are-in-the-world'. Only they don't notice that they are. It is something that has to be revealed to them. The point, then, in my opinion, isn't so much to acquire new feelings as to plumb the human condition more deeply.

What seems really important to me is that, at the point when Gaston Bachelard is attempting, through psychoanalysis, to identify the meanings our 'material imagination' lends to air, water, fire and earth, Ponge, for his part, is attempting to reconstruct them synthetically. There is in this encounter something like a promise to take the inventory as far as possible. And the only evidence I need that Ponge has succeeded fully wherever he has tried his hand at this are the multiple resonances evoked within me by his most successful passages. I shall cite at random the following lines on the snail:

> Snails . . . are fond of humid earth. Go on, they advance at full length, adhering to it all the way. They lug some along, they eat some, excrete some. They traverse it. It traverses them. This is interpenetration in the best of taste, tone on tone you might say—with one passive element, one active, the passive nourishing as it bathes the active . . .[76]

76 Ponge, 'Snails', in *The Nature of Things*, p. 27. (I have ignored the

These lines put me in mind irresistibly of a fine, grim passage from Malraux describing a dead woman at Toledo:

> Ten yards below a woman lay on the slope, one arm extended and the other clasping her head; he could clearly see the crisp, dark curls. She might have been asleep (but her head was pointing towards the bottom of the valley), were not the body under the flimsy dress flatter than any living woman's, and welded to the soil by the peculiar earthward impulse of the dead.[77]

Beyond the dead woman and the snail here, I sense a sort of relationship with the earth, a certain sense of fusion, of flattening, a relation of everything to death, to a mineralization of corpses. Everything is there in Ponge, superimposed.

Admittedly, you have to be careful not to *put* into the thing what you will subsequently claim to have *found* in it. Ponge hasn't always avoided this error. It is for this reason that I am less fond of his Washing Boiler. In that poem, he writes:

> Admittedly, I will not go so far as to claim that the example or lesson of the washing boiler should genuinely galvanize my reader—but I

misprint in Sartre's original French transcription of this poem [Trans.]).

77 André Malraux, *Days of Hope* (Stuart Gilbert and Alastair MacDonald trans.) (Harmondsworth: Penguin, 1970), pp. 122–3.

would no doubt feel a little contempt for him if he didn't take it seriously.[78]

In short, this is that lesson:

The washing boiler is designed in such a way that, when filled with a pile of filthy fabrics, the inner emotion and boiling indignation it feels at them, channelled toward the upper part of its being, falls back down as rain on this pile of filthy fabrics that sickens it—quasi- perpetually—and this leads to a purification.[79]

I fear I may be one of those contemptible readers who don't take the lesson at all seriously. How can we but see that what we have here is purely and simply a metaphor? Do we need a washing boiler to give body to this schema of purification that is present in everyone's mind and whose origins go back much further and are much more deeply rooted in us? And then the comparison is inexact, even from the standpoint of simple observation: it isn't the presence of dirty linen that heats up the water in the boiler. Without the heat from the hearth, that water would remain inert and would gradually grow dirty without effectively washing the clothes. And Ponge ought to know this better than anyone, since he was the one who put the boiler on the fire.

But there are so many other passages in which Ponge

78 Ponge, 'La lessiveuse', in *Pièces*, p. 75.
79 Ponge, 'La lessiveuse', in *Pièces*, p. 75.

reveals to us both the behaviour of things and, at the same time, our own behaviour, that his art seems to us, as is usually the case, to go further than his thought. For Ponge the thinker is a materialist[80] and Ponge the poet— if we leave aside the regrettable intrusions of science— has laid the foundations of a Phenomenology of Nature.

December 1944

---

80 But a genuine materialist will never write *Le Parti pris des choses*, since he will have recourse to Science and Science calls, a priori, for radical exteriority or, in other words, for the dissolution of all individuality. Now, what Ponge needs to petrify are, precisely, the countless significant individualities he finds around him. In short, he wants the world, as it is, to be eternalized.

＊

A NOTE ON SOURCES

'Black Orpheus'

Originally published as 'Orphée noir' in *Situations III*, NEW EDN (Paris: Gallimard, 2003), pp. 169–214.

First published in English translation in *The Aftermath of War* (London: Seagull Books, 2008), pp. 259–329.

'Man and Things'

Originally published as 'L'homme et les choses' in *Situations I* (Paris: Gallimard, 1947), pp. 226–70.

First published in English translation in *Critical Essays* (London: Seagull Books, 2010), pp. 383–485.